Ripeness is all!

the·ripest
moments

For George,
who knows
the beauty
of the landscape—
& his family.

Norbert Krapf
Indianapolis
3 June 2008

the• ripest moments

a southern Indiana childhood

Norbert Krapf

Indiana Historical Society Press
Indianapolis 2008

Printed in Canada

This book is a publication of the
Indiana Historical Society Press
Eugene and Marilyn Glick Indiana History Center
450 West Ohio Street
Indianapolis, Indiana 46202-3269 USA
www.indianahistory.org
Telephone orders 1-800-447-1830
Fax orders 1-317-234-0562
Online orders @ http://shop.indianahistory.org

The paper in this publication meets the minimum requirements
of American National Standard for Information Sciences—Permanence
of Paper for Printed Library Materials,
ANSI Z39. 48–1984

Library of Congress Cataloging-in-Publication Data

Krapf, Norbert, 1943-
  The ripest moments : a southern Indiana childhood / Norbert Krapf.
     p. cm.
  ISBN-13: 978-0-87195-262-2 (cloth : alk. paper)
 1. Krapf, Norbert, 1943—Childhood and youth. 2. Krapf, Norbert,
1943—Family. 3. Krapf, Norbert, 1943—Homes and haunts--Indiana.
4.
Poets, American—20th century—Biography. 5.
German-Americans—Biography. 6. Indiana—Social life and customs—
20th
century. I. Title.
  PS3561.R27Z46 2008
  811'.54--dc22
  [B]   2007044288

A publication from the Eli Lilly Indiana History Book Fund

To my parents, Clarence and Dorothy Schmitt Krapf,
my brothers and sister, Ed, Len, and Mary,
all the people whose names I mention,
and the unnamed who are a part of the story.

"And even if you were in a prison whose walls wouldn't admit to your senses any of the sounds of the outside world—wouldn't you, even so, still have your childhood, that precious, royal possession, that treasure-house of memories?"

Rainer Maria Rilke, *Letters to a Young Poet*
Tr. N. Krapf

"The first definitions, the fruits of the primary glances, can never be supplanted, for the trees of one's childhood are the touchstones of all later trees."

Allan Seager, *The Glass House*

Contents

Acknowledgments

"The Martin Box" originally appeared in *Confrontation*, "The Labor Day Boxes" in the *Indiana German Heritage Society Newsletter*, "The Gray Motorola" and "The Night the Game Was Called" in *The Southern Indiana Review*, and "The Parish Picnic" in *Traces of Indiana and Midwestern History*.

The author thanks the editors of these publications for permission to reprint the chapters listed above; his wife, Katherine, for listening to his questions, answering many of them, and catching most of his mistakes; his children, Elizabeth and Daniel, for their interest and curiosity; Stewart Rafert for his encouragement and support; John Fierst, local historian par excellence, for his inspiration in the classroom, work behind the scenes, and friendship over the years; the late Jack London Leas for the ironic and companionable inspiration to become a writer; and the New York Hoosier John Groppe for the stimulating questions, sustained faith, and support.

Anyone wishing to find materials relating to this memoir should know that the author donated his collection of family history papers, documents, and memorabilia from grade school, Boy Scouts, high school, and college to the Dubois County Museum in his hometown, Jasper, Indiana.

Preface

When you grow up as I did, the story of your childhood is also the story of a place, a community, and a time. I was born in 1943, in Jasper, Indiana, a German-Catholic town in the hills of southern Indiana. Not until years later, when I moved far away, to the East Coast, did I discover that my mother's and father's families came to Dubois County in 1840 and 1846, from a town and villages some twenty miles apart in Lower Franconia, in northern Bavaria. Few of us then, not long after World War II, had any command of the genealogical details, but many if not most of my Jasper relatives, friends, and acquaintences had a similar background. We were one generation removed from the farm, two or three generations removed from Germany, and a hundred years beyond the wilderness, still more of a presence to us than we could have seen or said.

My title, *The Ripest Moments*, is a metaphor drawn from nature, from gardening, from agriculture, that suggests how I approached these recollections of my rural, small-town childhood. Behind this book and my collections of poetry is a conviction that an awareness of individual and collective origins can enlighten, nourish, guide, and sustain us and those who come after us. In looking back at the time when I was a small child, through the eighth grade, with a few flashes to experiences and activities that extended into the years beyond, I have written about those memories that insistently rose to the surface.

I made no attempt to cover, sequentially, a particular period of time, either in my own life or in the life of my community or nation, but let those episodes, those memories of people and places lodged deepest within me, signal what I should write about. The story that I tell, however, is as communal as it is individual. I grew up as part of a community in which it often seemed that most people I knew were relatives, part of an extended system of clans. I was blessed to have more than one mother and father and kin who were not blood relatives.

If these memoirs describe the experience of readers of any generation and places other than the distinctive place and culture in which I was born and grew up, I am a happy writer. I have always believed that any story set deeply in one time and place, if told well, speaks for other times, places, and people. To put it another way, a sense of time and place travels and settles well. A life lived deeply anywhere resonates beyond the context of its specifics.

Although I have arranged the forty-two short chapters in a more or less chronological order, I did not write these chapters in the order in which they appear in the book. I was at the service of memory, a close kin to imagination. Although I have tried to be as accurate as possible, I recognize that someone else, even from my family, may tell his or her story, set in the same time or place, in a different way, from a different perspective, and come to different conclusions.

In the end, it is the intensity and skill in the telling of any life that captures our attention, speaks to our concerns, enlarges our capacity to see and feel, and helps us overcome whatever differences we thought may separate us from others. William Wordsworth, who celebrated "spots of time" in a famous autobiographical poem, tells us that "the child is father to the man." I have taken pleasure in reacquainting myself with the child who was father to the man I became and am glad for the opportunity to share these ripest moments of childhood.

1

The Music of the Grandfathers

About my grandfathers, all I can give you is stories I was told and one memory I carry with me.

My mother's father, Frank Schmitt, died when she was six years old. There were six children in the family, the oldest of whom was Alfred, my godfather, who was then twelve. The others were Frieda, William, Dorothy (my mother), Stella, and Betty. Grandma Mary Schmitt raised the six children by herself on a farm west of Ireland, Indiana, with no support from and little contact with the Schmitt family. I have seen pictures of Grandpa Frank, who died in 1919, twenty-four years before I was born. He was handsome, parted his hair in the middle, and played the mandolin. He was also a tenor and sang in the Saint Mary Parish choir. Mom said that he sang "Silent Night" beautifully in German: "Stille Nacht, heilige Nacht." Sometimes, on cold winter nights, Grandma and Grandpa and their six children sat around the wood-burning stove

in the parlor while he picked his mandolin and sang songs.
Grandma and Grandpa's wedding took place in 1906, the
first wedding mass ever celebrated in Saint Mary Catholic
Church. According to Mom, her daddy had consumption,
the doctor told him to take walks, he took one on a bitterly
cold and breezy day, the consumption worsened, and he
died. At his burial, Grandma Hoffman, who could not
have been a very happy person, pointed to the hole in the
ground where they were burying her son-in-law and said to
the six desolate children: "Look, your daddy is dead. They
are putting him in this hole and you won't ever see him
any more!" Mom cried when she told me this story in her
eighties, not long before she died.

Grandpa Frank's mandolin stayed in a closet in the
farmhouse after he died and eventually fell apart after
children and grandchildren played with it as a toy. When
Mom was a little girl, she slept with Aunt Frieda in the
upstairs bedroom on a mattress of corn shucks. Through
cracks in the roof Mom could sometimes see stars at night,
and sometimes snowflakes fell through those cracks and
landed on her face. She always liked country music and
from her I picked up a love of songs that feature mandolin
accompaniment. Any time I hear the mandolin, I also hear
a tenor voice singing, and I see a farmhouse and a young
mother and six young children.

Grandpa Benno Krapf had a handlebar mustache and
operated a steam-engine sawmill and threshing machine
in and around the village of Saint Henry, Indiana. I have

seen pictures of him watching the whirling circular saw of his sawmill cut into the white meat of logs and believe I inherited from him a love of the look, texture, feel, and grains of wood. Grandpa played the trumpet and also the violin. He grew fruit trees—apple, pear, and apricot—in his orchard behind the house he built on the hill near the cemetery. He also had a grape arbor and made his own wine, which my dad loved to sip. They called that house "The Sears & Roebuck" house because Grandpa purchased its design from a catalog. In 1910 he cut for free the timber for the new Saint Henry parish church, located on the other side of the cemetery in which he is buried. Also buried there is my Uncle Jerome Krapf, who died March 18, 1945, in Germany, so near the end of World War II. Uncle Jerome had been a seminarian at Saint Meinrad Archabbey for five years before he dropped out because of emotional strain. After he left Saint Meinrad, Uncle Jerome worked with Indian children at Saint Paul's Mission in South Dakota, where he received a draft notice. Grandpa Benno died of a heart attack less than three years after his son, Jerome, was killed by shrapnel in Germany. I think Uncle Jerome's death broke my grandfather's heart. My father's voice always trembled when he talked about Uncle Jerome's death.

Once, when I was two, we visited Grandma Mary and Grandpa Benno Krapf in their beautiful house in Saint Henry, which Grandpa built for his wife and family of ten children: Edgar, Flora (my godmother), Verena, Clarence

OPPOSITE PAGE, CLOCKWISE FROM BOTTOM, LEFT: Benno and Mary Luebbehusen Krapf wedding picture, 1897; "The Sears & Roebuck" home built circa 1914 by Grandpa Benno in Saint Henry; the wedding picture of Frank and Mary Schmitt with attendants Magdalena Schmitt and John Hoffman, standing, 1906; and Dorothy Schmitt Krapf, front left, and siblings after their father's early death: Alfred, center; Frieda, right; and Stella, Bill, and Betty in back.

ABOVE: Grandpa Benno's sawmill. Left to right: Joe Geeshen, Fritz Jochum, Theodore Wendholt, Benno Krapf, and Joseph Jochem. INSET: Grandpa Frank Schmitt, butchering.

(my father), Cornelius, Alfred (Fritz), Louise, Arthur (Shorty), Jerome, and Rita. I don't remember what time of year it was, maybe late summer or very early fall. I remember it was warm and the light was spectacular. There was a chicken pen partway down the hill, and Grandpa took me for a walk down the hill, opened the chicken pen gate, and led me by the hand inside so that we could visit with the chickens. What I remember most, what has stayed with me for decades, is that Grandpa Benno's hand was so warm and tender.

Grandma and Grandpa Krapf had a white-oak rocker that my father inherited. Dad always kept it in the living room of our new house. I remember that when he came back from having shock treatment at Our Lady of the Peace Hospital in Louisville, Kentucky, Dad sat in this rocker and rocked back and forth. From my seat on the couch, I could see that he was crying in silence. When Mother died, I chose this white-oak rocker as part of my inheritance. She had told me that in the house he built in Saint Henry, Grandpa Benno sat in this rocker and held me as a baby in his arms, rocking back and forth. When I sit in this rocker today, I see faces and hear lots of stories.

Basically, I grew up without grandfathers, except for what my parents shared with me about their fathers in the stories they told me. I had a number of great uncles on my mother's side of the family, however, and they were always kind to me. When you grow up in a community such as the German-Catholic community of Jasper, Indiana, at the time when I was a boy, you have countless blood relatives and a number of grandfather figures. What I missed most about not having a grandfather, though, is the stories my grandfathers could have told me about their parents and grandparents and about my mother and father.

Stories are what we share with one another to keep our parents and grandparents alive through the generations. This has been the story of a mandolin and a steam-engine sawmill and a boy who will always love songs with mandolins in them and the sound of tenor voices and the look and feel of the grains in woods such as cherry, walnut, white oak, and maple.

2

The Combine Calls

It was a bright, sunny summer day, the Fourth of July, and my mother and my brother Ed and I were sitting on the screened-in porch of our house at 415 East Fifteenth Street, Jasper, Indiana. I was four. Both Mom and Dad had grown up in the country, often told us stories about their rural childhood, and I was fond of going back to the farm. This usually meant the Schmitt farm on which my mother had grown up to the west of Jasper, three miles beyond the village of Ireland.

I'm not sure where my father was that summer holiday, perhaps helping a brother with a carpentry project, but he was certainly not with us on the porch. He and Mom had promised to take me and Ed that day to the farm, where our relatives were going to combine wheat—a big event in my eyes, an extravaganza. I wanted to go very badly and began to lose my patience when nothing happened on the porch. We just sat there, swinging back and forth as the chains went "squeak, squeak, squeak."

Finally, I could not take it any more and took matters in my own hands—or feet, as it were. I was barefoot, so it was not difficult to pad softly to the screen door, walk nonchalantly to the sidewalk, turn left, and begin to walk toward the vacant lot on the corner. My cousins Jim and Junior (Otto) Hoffman lived about a half-mile away. I knew they were going "down to the farm," and I did not want to be left out of the fun. Their mother, my Aunt Frieda, was a second mother to me. She and her husband, Otto Hoffman, bought land adjacent to the Schmitt farm that they allowed the relatives to cultivate, and Jim and Junior had more opportunities to go to the farm than I did. I knew they were going that day, envied their good luck, and was determined to be part of the festivities.

Once I passed the vacant lot and crossed the first street, I knew I could go all the way. We kids spent most of the summer without shoes. By that time of the season, the soles of my feet were pretty tough, and I just kept chugging along. I remember that the streets and sidewalks were very hot and there was lots of sticky tar to avoid. I climbed one hill, went down the other side, and crossed to the far side of Fifteenth Street at the intersection with Main Street, where the abandoned Wilson's Green House, in front of which shards of glass glittered in the gutter, stood in a shambles.

After I crossed the street, I somehow stepped on a piece of glass and cut my foot, but not bad enough to stop

At thirty-seven months, 1946.

me from reaching the end of my journey. Nobody, not *nothing*, was going to stop me from seeing my cousins Pat, Frank, and Mike Schmitt combine wheat. I wanted to hear the tractors and the combine roar, the gears grind, the men shout, and the wheat rumble into the wagons.

When I got to Newton Street, the busy and dangerous north and south route through town (US 231), I looked both ways, crossed, chugged up the hill to Aunt Frieda's limestone house at the top, and turned in the driveway. I tried to keep from limping, because if they saw I was injured, I knew they'd never bring me along. Maybe they'd take me to the hospital instead. Aunt Frieda, who could be stern, grinned when she saw me and listened to what I said about where I wanted to go and what I *had* to do.

"I'll call your Mom," she said.

"Dorothy," she said when my mother answered the phone, "Do you know where Norb is?"

"Sure, he's right here?"

"Can you see him?"

"Just a minute, I'll go check." She came back and admitted that she could not find me. "Maybe he's down in the vacant lot with the other kids."

"No, Dorothy, he's here," Frieda told her younger sister. "He said you promised to take him down to the farm to see the combining, aren't going, and he wants to come with us. Is it okay? Otto and I will be glad to bring him."

Probably because she was so relieved that I was safe, Mom gave permission for me to drive down to the farm

CLOCKWISE FROM BOTTOM: With my brother, Ed, on tricycles, ready to roll in front of our East Fifteenth Street home; with my parents visiting relatives in Louisville, 1944; Krapf and Hoffman cousins on the Newton Street slide; and with Aunt Frieda Schmitt Hoffman and her sons, Otto Jr. and Jim.

with her sister and family. Aunt Frieda, a nurse, cleaned and put some hydrogen peroxide and a Band-Aid on my wound, I scrambled into the car with my cousins, and we drove to the farm. I was thrilled to be able to watch my older cousins Pat, Frank, and Mike operate the farm machinery and send dusty streams of golden brown wheat cascading into the wagons that lurched away down the lane.

That was the first and last time I ever ran away from home.

3

The Art of Frugality

When my godfather Alfred Schmitt's children were young, Grandma Mary Schmitt spent a lot of time with them on the farm, the old homestead where she raised my mother and five other children. My grandfather died at the age of thirty-three, when Uncle Alfred, the oldest, was twelve, and any woman with the responsibility of pulling a fatherless family of six through the Great Depression knew that frugality was an essential part of a good upbringing. Grandma wanted to pass on this virtue to her grandchildren.

As so often happens, however, when an experienced person with graying hair tries to impress upon members of a later generation the lessons life has taught her, youth resists. In this case, the youth was Pat Schmitt, my godfather's oldest son, my first cousin, then age five or six. Eventually Pat, with another brother, took over the Schmitt dairy farm.

Grandma, who was spending several weeks with Alfred and his family, was worried that Pat or his younger brother, Frank, might set the farmhouse or barn on fire while playing with matches. Using her grandmotherly instincts, she devised a strategy to prevent them from playing with fire.

"Patty," she said, with a stern, matronly look on her face, "you know how poor we are. We haff to save. We chust haff to save on *effry*thing. We *haff* to save matches, especially because they are hard to get. We need them to light the stove in the kitchen and the living room. If you find some matches anywhere, you chust bring them to me. Okay?"

"*Ja*, okay," Pat replied, but there came a time when the oft-repeated warning began to grate on his young German sensibility and kindled the spark of rebellion.

One day Pat was playing near the stove in the living room and found a box of stick matches that Uncle Alfred had left behind after lighting the morning fire before leaving for the fields. As the boy fingered the box, he imagined what power it would give, what a great pleasure it would be, to make flame by striking one of the matches. Grandma's warning ran through his mind, but his earlier "*Ja*" quickly turned to a resolute "*Nein!*" He took out a match from the box and was about to rub it against the side when Grandma walked into the room, aghast at what she saw.

"Ach, you *bad* boy, Patty!" she growled. "How many times have I told you we *haff* to save matches? Don't you remember how many times I told you we must save? Chust give them here!" As she took the match and matchbox from his retreating hands, shaking her head and clucking her tongue, my cousin's temper flared. His reply has become a family legend.

"Grandma," he piped, eyes ablaze, "save, *shit*, save!"

4

Grandma Schmitt's House on North Main

After Uncle Alfred, her oldest son, married and took over the farm near Ireland, Indiana, Grandma Mary Schmitt bought a small house on north Main Street in Jasper, just a few minute's walk from Aunt Frieda's stone house on Newton Street. Every Thanksgiving and often at Christmas, the Schmitt clan would gather at Grandma's little house. Uncle Freddie and Aunt Stella Prechtel, with their children Fred Jr., Mary Frances, Bill, Phyllis, Gene, and Ray, and Uncle Louie and Aunt Betty Schwartz, with their children Donna, Johnny, and Larry, drove in from Louisville. Uncle Alfred's children Pat, Frank, Mike and Mary Ann, who were older than us, would come with their spouses and then their children. Uncle Bill and Aunt Lucy Schmitt brought Howard, Ken (Ace), Nancy, Alan, Connie, and Janie. Aunt Frieda and Uncle Otto Hoffman, while he was still alive, brought Otto Junior, Jim, who was my age, Sara, and Charles, whom Uncle Otto had named "Humpty"

and "Schneebrunzer" (Snowwhizzer). Mom and Dad
brought me, Ed, Lenny, and Mary Lou.

We were an energetic, noisy, irrepressible brood of
cousins in a little house too small to contain us all at one
time, unless we were all eating, the sacrament that bound
us together. Seated at card tables set up in the basement,
around the oak table and on extra folding chairs against the
walls in the kitchen, and on the sofa or chairs in the living
room, we fit together at the meal like a closed accordion.
In the summers, our Schmitt gatherings were usually at
Grandma's Lake on the Schmitt farm near Ireland, but at
Thanksgiving and Christmas Grandma's Jasper house was
the center of festivities. The food that I associate with those
happy occasions is baked turkey, the skin dark brown and
stuffed with bread dressing; dark gravy; mashed potatoes;
sweet potatoes; brussels sprouts; corn; and cranberry relish.
For dessert, there were pumpkin and squash pies, with a
scoop of vanilla ice cream on top or the side. Nobody was
ever limited to one helping of anything; we got to go back
for as many servings as we wanted.

The children always ate first, a smart move on the
part of the adults. Then we bolted through the door to
play outside while the aunts and uncles sipped homemade
wine or beer and caught up with one another's family
developments and local gossip. If the weather was mild,
as it sometimes was at Thanksgiving, we played outside
in our sweaters. We ran like released inmates all over
the neighborhood, shrieking, shoving, gyrating, jumping

Grandma Schmitt, who died at age ninety-four.

up and down, jabbing, pointing, and teasing one another
with barely concealed affection. Our favorite games were
kick-the-tin-can and hide-and-seek, but sometimes the
boys might toss a football or dribble a basketball on the
sloping North Main Street, to see if we could prevent it
from observing the rules of gravity. If we got together at
Grandma's at Easter, as we sometimes did, then some of
us played pitch and catch in the rock driveway or on the
street. The neighbors' lawns and backyards were supposed
to be off limits, but we could not contain ourselves during
the heat of a game and often transgressed our limits. The
one exception was the yard of the next-door neighbor,
the heavyset, gentle, and elderly Mrs. Vogel. Because our
parents told us that her doctor made her drink pig's blood
for some kind of deficiency, we cut her more than a little
slack, even though she was sweet when she said hello.

During the winter, Grandma, a widow who raised
six preteen children by herself on the farm, kept the
living room closed off and unheated, but for these
festive occasions the room was open and warm, a central
attraction. On a table in one corner was a glass rose-colored
coal oil lamp from the farm that had been electrified,
and on a table in the opposite corner was her miniature
artificial Christmas tree, with its unique bubbling colored
electric candles, so interesting they could even make you
sit there and look at them for a minute or two. Another
main attraction was the Christmas cactus that bloomed
only at that time of year. Every Christmas, one of my aunts

or uncles posed Grandma, smiling, in front of this cactus in bloom and took a snapshot that we had reprinted and shared.

One of the special treats a grandchild could get in Grandma's house when your family paid a nonholiday visit was a buttered slice of the white bread she baked on occasion, so moist, soft, and light but substantial, that you always wanted another piece. I can still see the bread knife cutting a slice on the board, the butter spreading across its width and breadth and melting as I lifted the home-baked viaticum to my mouth. If Grandma ever made a mistake and cut a slice too thin or spilled a drink she was serving, she always said, "Oh pshaw!" Her other favorite expressions were "Mercy!" and "Hea–vuns!" She called me "Nor–butt."

Whenever our family came for a visit, Grandma always served us a soda in the kitchen. We would sit around the circular oak table she had brought along with her to Jasper from the farm, light would stream in the window on Mrs. Vogel's side of the house, and Grandma would stand at the counter, her back to us, preparing the drinks. She lined up three or four glasses, depending on how many of us came along, and was always determined to pour exactly the same amount of 7 Up in each glass. Just before she placed the glasses on a tray to turn around and bring them to the table, she would stoop and eyeball the levels of soda one more time, lift one glass, and dump some of it into somebody else's glass.

Grinning, she stepped slowly toward us with the tray of

drinks and snacks. To Grandma Schmitt, all grandchildren were equal under the eternal law and must be served exactly the same amount of soda. We could have as many of her sugar cookies as we wanted, but the soda had to be equal.

Years later, after a series of strokes rendered Grandma an invalid and she died at the age of ninety-four, I learned from her obituary that she had ninety grandchildren and great-grandchildren. When I expressed my amazement over the size of our clan, my mother informed me that I was the only one of the ninety who conversed with Grandma in German, which I did not begin to speak until I was almost thirty.

5

Summers on the Farm

Summers I often got to spend a week or two on the farm where my mother grew up, with Uncle Alfred Schmitt, my godfather, and his family. Aunt Elizabeth Schmitt was a good cook who served such meals as round steak with dark gravy, mashed potatoes, fresh green beans, peas or carrots, sliced tomatoes, and Bibb lettuce (picked from the vegetable garden behind the house) doused with hot bacon drippings and sprinkled with sugar. Under a sugar maple in the side yard, there was a well. You used a handle to draw up a bucket of cold water, which you sipped from a tin ladle. Hollyhocks grew tall near that old farmhouse, along with sweet peas, marigolds, and peonies.

Opposite the house was the barn in which I loved to lose myself in the thick daytime darkness. Flies swarmed in the hot air and the smell of cow dung drifted up to the hayloft from the stalls below. To the side of the house was the smokehouse, in which curing hams hung. In a corner were barrels of wine (elderberry, grape, Virginia

Dare, his specialty, and sometimes blackberry) that Uncle
Alfred made. Close scrutiny revealed at least one jug of
moonshine stashed away. Above the first floor, where
the curing and smoking was done, was a loft which Mike
Schmitt, my cousin and pal, and I explored one rainy day.
We found an old gramophone with a speaker cone and a
bulldog logo. Another building that I enjoyed exploring was
the granary, beneath which my mother played as a child. In
the summer heat, I loved the smell of dry grain and dried
shucked ears of corn from the previous harvest.

Around the barnyard, in which at least one red Case
tractor (one had big metal spiked wheels in the back) was
always parked, stood several big-leaved catalpa trees, whose
long "beans," as we called them, swayed in the breeze.
Uncle Alfred, a good fisherman, liked to use catalpa worms
as bait. A throwback to the days before the combustion
engine, an old plowhorse named Charlie was still part of
the menagerie. Charlie loved to lounge in the shade of
those catalpas. Sometimes Mike and I would hitch a sled
up behind Charlie and let him pull some hay out into the
pasture for the cows. More often, Mike would drive the
topless red Jeep, stack one bale on the left fender, one on
the right, race along the lane toward where the cows were
huddled, swerve as he hit the brakes, let one bale go flying,
back up, pick up some speed, and turn another "Cat's ass"
so that the other bale would also go flying. Those cows
had to wonder what in tarnation the two young two-legged
steers were up to.

My mother with her godson, my cousin, Mike Schmitt, on the farm at his First Communion.

My children, Elizabeth and Daniel, posing on a tractor at the farm, 1987.

One of my favorite chores on the farm was bringing the cows in for milking in the late afternoon. Mike and I, sometimes accompanied by Uncle Alfred, would walk down the rock road barefoot to the pasture near the lake about a quarter mile away to gather and lead the herd to the barn. When we walked or jogged in the pasture, we had to be careful where we put our feet down, unless we did not care what might squish up between our toes. Once, Uncle Alfred was with us and wanted us to hurry along. Maybe it was getting a bit late for the cows to be milked, maybe he had somewhere to go that evening, but he was clearly in a rush. "Norbert!" he blurted, "run faster after those cows. Run like hell, like you're hitting a home run!" "Sheesh!" I thought, "he's used to country baseball, to 'pasture ball,'" a variety my father had also played in his youth in Saint Henry. "In Jasper, the big city, we have fences in our ballpark," I wanted to tell him, but didn't. We hit the ball over the fence and we get to "run" around the bases in a loping trot. But I did run like hell, to please my godfather.

During my earliest summer visits on the farm, my cousin Frank, who was older than Mike, did the milking, literally, by hand. Country music by Hank Williams and Hank Snow and others, with fiddles slurring and steel-pedal guitars weeping, twanged and pulsed out of a tiny radio on a shelf above the concrete floor where Frank sat on a stool, pulling and squeezing cow teats and splashing warm milk on the side of a pail to the beat of songs about cheatin' hearts, no-tell motels, and busted relationships.

Flies feasted in the witch's brew of an atmosphere until a brown tail lashed them off their perch.

One day the phone rang, the oldest of my cousins, Pat Schmitt, answered it, and he headed out the door in a full run and out of the barnyard at breakneck speed in the red Jeep. Aunt Justine, who lived just up the highway, at an angle across the fields, was threatening to jump into the cistern again. When Pat approached the point where the rock road intersected with the highway, he barely slowed down as he made a left turn, tires squealing. Later he drove back down the rock road at a more leisurely pace, pulled into the barnyard, hit the brakes, and skidded to a stop. "They got her to stop," he announced, and went back brusquely to his chores.

The most bucolic activity of those summer days on the farm was walking with Mike down the lane beside a fencerow to the little woods a few hundred yards behind the house, roaming beneath the pawpaw, dogwood, maple, oak, and ash trees. It was in these woods that my mother was expected to go, every day, as a little girl to stir the corn mash in the still. Another highlight was the time Mike was allowed to drive me in the pickup on a Saturday night to Velpen, a hamlet of a few houses, where we bought soda and potato chips and sat in the truck and watched a Ma and Pa Kettle movie projected onto the white clapboards on the side of the general store. After the movie was over, all the drivers facing that wooden "screen," including Mike, honked their horns. Two or three of the vehicles made a sound like this: "Aroooga, arooooga, aroooooga!"

It was also fun to try to shimmy up the twin sugar maple trees, kept closely trimmed, that stood before the front porch. Later Mom told me that her older sister, Aunt Frieda Hoffman, a second mother to me, had been a big tattletale. "She always tried to get me in trouble," Mom insisted, "and told Mom I didn't do my work." So one day young Dorothy, whom my cousins called Aunt Dots, finished her chores, snuck out of the house with a book in her hand, climbed up one of those maples, found herself a nice comfortable place to sit, where she was not visible from below, and read the poems of James Whitcomb Riley. Aunt Frieda kept circling the house trying to find her little sister goofing off somewhere in the yard, garden, or behind one of the farm buildings. Fuming big sister Frieda never did catch little sis Dots, perched on a branch, chuckling to herself as she read dialect poetry about Little Orphant Annie.

6

Sundays at the Lake

It was really a pond, the construction of which was financed by the government as a water conservation project, a reservoir, but we called it "The Lake." It was built on land owned by Grandma Schmitt and farmed by Uncle Alfred Schmitt and his sons Pat and Frank, a quarter mile down the road from the farmhouse. There was a sense in which it belonged to all of us, or so we felt, even though Alfred was the supervisor and caretaker and had stocked the waters with bass, catfish, channel cats, perch, and bluegill.

Sometimes the whole clan, from Dubois County as well as those who had relocated during the Great Depression and married men from Louisville, Kentucky, gathered there on Sundays in the summer to eat, swim, splash, fish, go boating, listen to baseball games, eat and drink some more, and razz one another. If we were lucky, we kids might even get to spend the night in the school bus that

Aunt Frieda Hoffman, who loved to fish, had bought, put
up on blocks, and converted to a "cabin," furnished with
gas stove, cabinets, table, and beds. Across from the cabin,
just inside what was a cornfield, was Grandma Schmitt's
vegetable garden, which Mom and Aunt Frieda helped her
tend and harvest her crop of tomatoes, sweet corn, peas,
green peppers, green beans, carrots, cabbage, spinach, and
lettuce.

Being at The Lake on a Sunday in the summer was
like being in a Brueghel painting of children's games or a
wedding feast, or both combined. Everybody was doing
something full tilt, at the same time, at a slightly different
place, but was part of the whole picture. Mom, her sisters,
Frieda, Stella, and Betty (the last two from Louisville),
their sister-in-law Lucy, and Grandma warmed up the
food on the stove and carried hot dishes to a long table
under the maple tree, while Uncle Bill grilled hamburgers
or steaks next to Dad and Uncle Louie Schwartz, who
drank beer in their folding chairs and shot the breeze.
Meanwhile, my cousins Jim and Junior Hoffman and Alan
Schmitt and my brother Ed and I seined for minnows in
the creek near the road, or on another part of the farm, or
maybe checked the lines for channel cats in the aluminum
boat stored upside down during the week under the walnut
tree next to the outhouse. My cousins Sara Hoffman and
Nancy, Connie, and Janie Schmitt played board games or
did crafts or just joked and laughed with their cousins from
Louisville, Mary Frances and Phyllis Prechtel and Donna

Schwartz. I did not know how many first cousins I had because there were so many, and when you are rich you should not count all your individual dollars and blessings, you should feel good about what you have, can share and spend with others, and be grateful.

One of the aunts or Mom would yell, "Soup's on!" or "Come and get it" and we would all come running to the big long table to pick out from steaming dishes and pots whatever we craved, especially if our mother did not usually serve that at home. There was fried and baked chicken, roast beef, sometimes turkey, ham (the vowel of which the Kentuckians twisted to the delight of us Dubois County natives, causing us to cackle and imitate their accents), bread dressing, mashed potatoes and gravy, baked beans, green beans, peas (sometimes mixed with carrots), creamy cole slaw, sliced beefy tomatoes, sliced cucumbers soaked in a white dressing, and wilted Bibb lettuce overlayed with thin crescents of white onions. We piled our paper plates high until they bent and sagged, emptied them, came back for seconds and thirds, for more variety, and then got ready for dessert. We could pick from angel food cake; applesauce; German chocolate cake; apple, peach, rhubarb, or blackberry pie, any of which could be topped with ice cream; sometimes homemade fruit salad; and red and green Jell-O filled with cubed peaches, apples, and bananas.

Then it was time to "lay low" while the food settled. "You can't go swimming for at least an hour, or you'll all get

ABOVE: *In front of Aunt Frieda's "cabin" at Grandma's Lake, 1958: Ed, Len, and Mary Krapf; Sara and Charles Hoffman.* LEFT: *Jumping and swimming at "The Lake."*

cramps!" someone's mom always announced. "So take it easy."

During that "settling" period, some of us walked over the far dam to the "back lake," an L-shaped pond, the first part of which was on Grandma's property, the other on the neighboring farm. It was always quieter at the back lake, which had trees along one side, including a stand of pines whose carpet of needles made a nice mattress to lie down on for a good snooze. In the fall, Aunt Frieda, whose husband, Otto Hoffman, died young of a liver disease, leaving her to raise three children alone, shrewdly and skillfully pulled in handsome crappies with her fly rod in the shallows of this more remote lake. Aunt Frieda always knew how to do everything, because she had learned to fend for her family by herself.

After the rest period was over, we boys came back to the front lake, put on our swimming suits, swam across the lake to the diving board on the far side, and compared our diving abilities. The younger kids stayed in the shallow sand closer to the cabin, under a big sycamore tree, within range of several adults sitting on folding chairs or a blanket. We also took turns checking the "jugs," baited for channel cats and placed around the lake, with a rowboat, or just slipped inside an old inner tube and drifted wherever the breeze and our inclinations might take us. Later in the afternoon, one or two of us might cast for bass in a far corner of the lake where silence seemed concentrated.

Wherever you were, you could hear the voice of Harry Caray, who had a flare for theatrics, announcing the Saint Louis Cardinal game: "Base hit like a bullet to center field, tie game!" or, "Bottom of the ninth, Musial in his crouch, he swings, there she goes, all the way to the pavilion roof, home run, the Cardinals win, the Cardinals win, Holy Cow!" And the Chicago Cubs or Cincinnati Reds fans, the infidels among the family ranks, would groan and moan about how prejudiced Caray was.

Sometimes I liked to slip away by myself into the cornfield, crawl between rows of corn into a leafy cave where some sunlight splashed onto my head, and listen to the sounds of the family gathering. Or maybe I would sneak off to the back lake alone, lie down in the cool, sweet air of the pine grove, and listen to the turtle doves coo. No matter where you were at The Lake, no matter what you were doing, no matter whom you were with, you felt you were a part of the universal hum, the sacred togetherness of the place.

7

The Barn

In the summer, a barn is a warm womb. Uncle Alfred Schmitt's barn was warm, dark, quiet, secret, and secure. If you must work in the barn every day, it is something other than a womb, but for me and my cousins, the few times we had the barn to ourselves, it was a welcoming womb. Sometimes we would come over from The Lake, where we were having a Schmitt reunion, to the farmhouse where our mothers had grown up just to get away for a while. If our older cousins, Alfred's sons, were doing chores, feeding cattle or hogs, repairing a Case tractor, mending fences, or clearing out a ditch, we had the hayloft of the big barn all to ourselves, with no supervision in sight.

We entered by the main door, swung open wide, opposite the house and the maple tree, and scampered up the nearest perpendicular ladder to the loft. Hanging from a pulley before the opening where the hay bales came in on the escalator, in the little light visible in the entire loft, was a huge thick rope. We would grab it, shimmy up it, push ourself off with our feet against a stack of bales, and swing free. The idea was to swing back and forth enough times that your momentum built up and you could release yourself at just the right moment and land with a happy thump on a certain level or a selected recess padded with bales. We had a contest to see who could swing the highest and land the farthest away from the light. We would see who could swing the longest and creak the loudest before letting go, or see who could land on his feet and not fall over. Or maybe we would want to go two at a time and coordinate our release or let go one after another, and then start wrestling as soon as we hit the hay.

After swinging and leaping to our heart's content, we sometimes played hide-and-seek, mostly by fingertip and sound, in the daylight dark of this suspended kingdom of hay and straw. If everybody was hidden, the searcher could hear the drone of flies, the buzzing of bees, and the occasional meow of a kitten that had scratched and climbed its way into the loft. Sounds from the farmhouse and barnyard would drift your way. If you were really patient, a good hunter, you might even detect the inhaling and exhaling of a cousin in a narrow cave between two stacks of bales and notice every movement in the whole dark expanse, no matter how minute. The coo of a dove, the flutter of a wing, would seem monumental.

If you found the opportunity to be in the loft alone, you swam in a slow current of tranquility, reclining on your

ABOVE: *Daniel and Elizabeth in the Schmitt barn, 1987.*
INSET: *Introducing Daniel and Elizabeth to a calf.*

back, facing the escalator opening, and watching the rays of light slant onto the rough floorboards or bales of hay. You could see motes of dust riding those rays of light, and even the smell of cow shit rising from the stables below was sweet. There was no rush, no movement, no passage of time. You had not yet been born, existed prior to time. You did not want to move beyond where you were. You were not yet ready for human company. The bawling of a calf below was balm to your ear. The air was warm, moist, and you floated off to sleep.

When you awoke, you did not remember where you were. It was hard to rise to your feet and find your balance, and when you staggered out of the barn, the sun blinded you. It took a while before your vision readjusted, you recovered your step, and felt the impulse to shape words with your tongue.

8

The House on East Fifteenth Street

When I was born, Mom and Dad were renting part of
a house owned by the MacDonalds on the corner of East
Fifteenth and Vine streets, but soon we bought the house
next door, at 415 East Fifteenth Street. We lived in this
small house until I was nine years old, when we moved
to a new house we built on Schroeder Avenue in Holy
Family Parish, then outside the city limits. At the house
on Fifteenth Street, there was a small white picket fence
along the front of the side yard and the line dividing our lot
from the McDonald's. On this side of the house there was
a porch whose back was a trellis that in the summer was
thatched with Mom's Heavenly Blue Morning Glories. As
a little guy, I loved to pad barefoot down the porch steps,
shuffle across the dewy lawn, and gaze up at those open
blue passageways into eternity. The back of the property
backed on and dropped down sharply to George Kieffner's

vegetable garden. Kieffner's son Larry was a neighborhood pal who became a classmate.

In the front of the house was a screened-in porch with a swing, on which we spent a lot of time. For most of the time we lived in that house, Dad worked in a chair factory, and when he came home from work, my brother Ed and I liked to sit on that swing with him. After Dad joined the Krapf Insurance Agency with his brother Cornelius Krapf, he would come home for supper, then visit a client or two after the meal, come back home and have a beer. Sometimes he would let Ed and me have a sip. It was probably from those experiences that, taking Dad as our model, we learned to sigh in satisfaction after taking a good sip.

On a hot summer day when I was six, Mom, who did not drive, had to go shopping for groceries. Dad had to drive her, and so she left me there in charge of four-year-old Ed. We played ball out in the side yard, contained by the white picket fence, became hot after running the imaginary bases on the lawn and decided to go into the kitchen for a cool drink. After we finished what was left of a pitcher of cold lemonade, I found that my sizable thirst had not been quenched. What else could I drink? The only cold liquid I could find in the refrigerator was a bottle of beer. I grabbed it, found the opener, imitated the way Dad opened his bottle of Pabst Blue Ribbon or Oertel's or Sterling in the evening, tilted the opening into my mouth, and chugged away. I sat the empty bottle on the kitchen table,

ABOVE: *My second birthday: Hoffman cousins on left, cousins Elfrieda and Ronnie Schwinghamer on right.* LEFT: *With my father, Easter, 1946.*

and we rambled onto the porch, tripped down the steps, and strolled onto the lawn to play more games. I thought I had been pretty grown up.

When Mom came back from shopping, she and Dad carried bags of groceries into the kitchen, found an empty beer bottle standing there, all alone, on the kitchen table, and she called my name, emphatically. I came running, happy that they had come back home.

"How did this bottle of beer get emptied?" Mom asked, with a stern face.

"I drank it!" I admitted, rather proudly, thinking I was acting like quite the little man of the house. That set off a firestorm of a lecture. My father must have had a good chuckle on the sly over my imitation of what it meant for him to be the man of the house.

One time Ed, who was out in the side yard playing, did not want to come into the house when it was time to eat. "Norb," Mom said, "go out and coax him in."

"Okay," I said, but although I liked the sound of the word "coax," I did not know what it meant. So I went up to my little brother, tickled him on the chin, and said, "Coaxie, coaxie." He came in.

Another time Ed was playing out on the lawn near the sidewalk and Mrs. Collignon, our friend whose daughter, Clara Mae, was our babysitter, came walking along. I had been sick with the flu and Mrs. Collignon asked how I was doing. "Oh, Norb's OK," Ed piped up, "but Mom's got the shits!" Mrs. Collignon doubled over in laughter and came

Ed, age four, on a pony in the alley.

ABOVE: *Christmas greetings from 415 East Fifteenth Street, Jasper.* RIGHT: *Our first snowman.*

running into the house with tears in her eyes to tell Mom the story.

Several times during the summer an unshaven, scruffily dressed hobo would come to the front door, knock, and politely ask for "a bite to eat, please." These hoboes had walked along Fifteenth Street from the train tracks that ran along the eastern end of the street near Buffalo Swamp. I remember Mom making peanut butter and jelly sandwiches for them and giving them a cup of milk. "Thank you Ma'am," they always said.

After summer thunderstorms, there were always puddles on East Fifteenth Street that we jumped into and out of. The ice cream man came pushing a three-wheeled cart summer evenings and we all ran up to him to buy our nickle Fudgsicle®, Popsicle®, or Dreamsicle®. The best way to get the wrappers off them so you could start sucking and slurping as soon as possible was to loosen them, hold the bottom tight where the stick entered, and make a kind of hot-air balloon of the wrapper by blowing your breath inside. Summer afternoons there were baseball games in Adam Schmitt's vacant lot on the corner of East Fifteenth and Dewey streets. All the kids in the neighborhood from several streets away gathered in that vacant lot to play ball, to suck the juices of the plums when they ripened on the trees that stood in a row along the third base line, and to play kick-the-tin-can.

One summer I was picking weeds on the bank that descended from East Fifteenth Street down to that vacant lot. I was intrigued by one short weed whose stem ended with a cone shaped seed pack, stuck it in my nostril, and twirled it around. When the stem broke off leaving that cone of seeds wedged in my nostril, I ran home in a panic to Mom, who pulled it out with a tweezers. Decades later, I learned that the name of that weed was plantain. Another time I was trying to fly my kite in that lot. I ran down that bank pulling the kite behind me, tripped, and fell. Right where I fell there was a branch with a sharp end sticking out. I fell right on that sharp end, which punctured my hand so deeply you could almost see its point sticking out the back. I ran home howling, Mom and Dad took me to the doctor, and he pulled out that stake. Mom later wrapped it with a slab of bacon fat, tied strips of cloth around it, and when I went to school the next day with a note from her, my teacher, a nun, said, "Now you know how Jesus felt!" All I felt was stupid.

9

Adam Schmitt's Vacant Lot

Anyone born in Jasper has a good chance of being of German descent and having relatives in town and elsewhere in Dubois County. I could walk down the alley beside our house and in just a few minutes be at the home of Great-uncle Joe Hoffman and his wife Mame, born a Kreilein, and receive food, drink, and all the attention any child craves.

There were many children in the neighborhood, including Larry Kieffner, who lived around the corner, Gaylord and Ruth Schuch, Kenny Kreilein, the Newman sisters, the Kueblers and the Kleins, and we all had the perfect place to play at the corner of East Fifteenth and Dewey streets: Adam Schmitt's vacant lot. This lot, which had a row of plum trees on the side opposite Fifteenth Street, was sunken below the street so that there was a fairly steep bank sloping down to what was our playing field. Every evening, many afternoons, and most summer

mornings, we had a ball game on the diamond laid out
on this vacant lot. Home plate was in the back of the lot,
close to the house that was next to ours, first base was near
Fifteenth Street at the bottom of the hill, center field was
bounded by Dewey Street, and left field was just this side
of that marvelous row of old plum trees. Every spring when
we began to play our neighborhood games, those plum
trees were in profuse bloom. Foul balls would tear into the
blossoms and leaves, and on occasion a right-handed pull
hitter would thwack a line drive against the split bark of
one of the dark trunks.

In the summer, in the endless hot summer, when the
major league season was well under way and we knew the
batting averages of our favorite players and the standings
of all teams in either league, the plums took on a deeper
and darker shade and became softer. When they were soft
enough, and no adults were looking, we picked as many as
we could hold, bit into them, and let the warm, sugar-sweet
juice burst on our tongues. It was most fun when the juice
dripped from your chin onto your Adam's apple.

I heard at home that the mysterious Adam Schmitt, the
owner of the lot, was a distant relative, but I never met or
saw him. He must have operated a successful construction
company, however, for every once in a while the warning
cry "Adam Schmitt! Adam Schmitt!" broke up our baseball
game, a raid on those delicious fruit trees in foul territory,
or the kick-the-tin-can (can on home plate) we played after
it was too late for baseball. We hid behind a tree trunk or

TOP: *The East Fifteenth Street gang, circa 1947: Mary Lou Brang, left; Krapf brothers, center; and Newman sisters, right.* ABOVE, LEFT: *My First Communion, 1952, with my parents.* ABOVE, RIGHT: *With Uncle Ed Krapf and brother Ed at Grandma Krapf's Easter egg hunt, Wagner Street, Jasper, 1949.*

Top: Krapf father with sons, 1953, shortly before move to Schroeder Avenue. Above, Left: My First Communion, with godparents Flora Krapf Schwinghamer and Alfred Schmitt. Above, Right: Posing with my grandmothers at my First Communion.

bush or slipped into the alley next to the house behind home plate, as a big dump trunk roared and bounced down the street past the lot, spilling clods of southern Indiana dirt on the pavement. The doors were painted a dark green, right in the middle of which was scripted in white letters, "Adam Schmitt Construction." Part of the thrill of playing in the lot involved knowing we did not have the owner's permission and therefore were the equivalent of neighborhood bandits or vigilantes who reclaimed their land, their sacred territory, from an absentee landlord. Perhaps that is why those plums, brought to such an opulent sweetness by a democratic sun, tasted better than any other fruit I have ever eaten.

Sometime during the baseball season, when we were deep into a game alongside those plum trees, an old car pulled up at the curb of Fifteenth Street, a man some of us recognized as "The Horseradish Man" got out and opened his trunk, the game stopped, our sisters interrupted their hopscotch, someone yelled, "The horseradish man!" and parents came rushing to stand in line. It was as though the bishop, who appeared only once a year in the neighborhood, had come to our sacred outdoor church, and now it was time for all families to receive Holy Communion. That was the end of the baseball game for the day: we walked back home with our moms, dads, brothers, and sisters and the sacred plants whose roots we chopped and preserved to spice the meats we shared at our kitchen tables.

10

The Labor Day Boxes

When we lived on East Fifteenth Street, we children participated in a communal ritual that I have never seen performed elsewhere, or even heard about being practiced. Jasper was founded by Scotch-Irish Presbyterians in 1830, but before long a few German-Catholic families arrived, and when the energetic and ambitious Croation missionary Joseph Kundek followed in 1838 and went to work building his "German Catholic colony," as he called it, many of the Presbyterians moved on. Kundek's German-Catholic recruits brought with them to the new town in the hilly, densely forested wilderness their love of working with wood. Jasper's main industry is wood products, and the town prided itself on its reputation as "The Nation's Wood Capitol," as the misspelled sign on Rieder's Hill proclaimed to all who entered the town from the north. Many of our fathers worked in saw or planing mills or factories making plywood, chairs, desks, tables, various kinds of cabinets, and frames or chassis for Kimball pianos and organs. For twenty-five years, my father worked in a chair factory before joining an insurance agency his brother Cornelius had formed.

Kundek's German Catholics may also have introduced a tradition that was adapted to the local culture and industry of Jasper. In the German tradition schoolchildren created lanterns that were carried in a nocturnal procession celebrating Saint Martin's Day on November 11. This procession culminated in a pageant, in which the children performed, in pantomime, the story of Saint Martin of Tours, the aristocratic knight who, in a conversion ceremony of sympathy, cut his cloak in two with his sword and shared it with a beggar.

Labor Day was an important holiday in Jasper. The custom was for children to pull homemade Labor Day Boxes down the sidewalk at dusk. Our parents made the boxes for us, but allowed us to participate in their creation enough to feel that the results were, at least in part, of our own making. The simplest method was to take a cardboard shoe box, lift off the top, cut out squares or rectangles for windows on the long sides, and paste colorful, patterned crepe paper across them on the inside, giving the effect of stained-glass windows. In the middle of the box, you dripped some candle wax, set a small candle in it, allowed it to dry in place, then cut out a large hole in the lid and set it back on top. When the candle was lit, the red, blue, green, and gold stained-glass window glowed from within,

as though the Holy Spirit had come alive and was flickering
for all to see.

Dissatisfied with such flimsy construction, one year
our father got out his tools, selected a slab of thick leftover
plywood in his basement workshop, and made us wooden
Labor Day Boxes. We became the unofficial royalty of the
working-class neighborhood. Dad set our sturdy plywood
boxes on Tinker Toy axles and wheels, made a trap door
with a hinge on the top and a candleholder inside, and built
a long handle, which could bend and fold at a hinge in the
middle, for pulling our Tabernacle on Wheels. When we
pulled these custom-made deluxe models onto the concrete
sidewalk for the first time, as dusk descended on the maple
trees lining the streets and crickets sang their "Back To
School" song, my brother Ed and I felt equipped and
qualified to lead the parade of children.

We pulled our creations onto the sidewalk from our
property, turned right, and proceeded to the corner of
Fifteenth and Vine streets, which descended, gradually,
to where the factories began, and joined the stream of
children pulling their flickering boxes. Every neighborhood
had its own pageant and route. Adults stood in all the yards,
smiling, pointing, offering congratulations, sometimes
applauding. All the adults knew one another's children.
As we pulled, with pride, the boxes that our mothers and
fathers made, or helped us think we made, we chanted a
singsong litany that resounded up and down and back and
forth across the streets: "Labor Day, Labor Day! High High

Low, High High Low! Labor Day, Labor Day!" For an hour or two one evening every year, we were the center of creation. We possessed the voices to sing the sacred song, we had a loving audience, and in that festive atmosphere we honored the hard work of our fathers in the factories that fueled the local economy.

When the singing stopped, the parade ended, and the candlelight went out, we walked back to our houses with our parents, chatting in hushed voices, and stored our Labor Day Boxes for another year. After a reward of cake and ice cream, we went to bed full, tired, happy, and prepared to dream colorful candlelit dreams of solidarity with all the friends and relatives who worked so hard and knew how to share what they earned with those of us who would follow them.

11

The Hickory and the New House

For at least one year before our new house was built on Schroeder Avenue, in the Hasenour Addition, Mom and Dad had a vegetable garden on the property. Before a garden could be planted, however, many tree stumps had to be removed. When we bought the property, a logging company was still working in the woods beyond. Its path for removing the logs they had cut ran at an angle through our lot, beside where the garden was being laid out and through a section where the house Marcus Kuper built for us eventually stood. We had already bought the lot before the logging company finished clearing this route to the rock road that was Schroeder Avenue.

My father was delighted and proud that there was a young hickory tree near what became the corner of the garden. A man who had grown up hunting squirrels in the woods around the village of Saint Henry, he worshipped hickory trees and wanted to protect and cultivate that

lone hickory tree at all costs. One day we arrived at the
site to work in the garden and found fresh white wood
chips with truck tire tracks cut in the earth on either side
of them. The young hickory tree was gone, eliminated,
exterminated. I thought my father would break down and
cry uncontrollably. A very short, quiet, and gentle man with
a wickedly dry sense of humor who barely reached five feet
in height, he instead rose in stature in my eyes. He found
a way to express the fury that rose in and through him and
shot up as if propelled like a rocket by some mysterious
source of underground energy.

Dad ripped out a piece of lined paper from a small
notebook he kept in the glove compartment of the car,
wrote, as if with a scalpel, a short but terse note on it in
angry caps, and nailed the note to a stake. With a hatchet,
he chopped the bottom of that stake to a sharp point,
balanced a board with one hand on top of that stake, and
whacked the stake into the ground with the flat side of
the hatchet. There, in the middle of their "road," on our
property, stood my father's sign to the loggers, who had
dared to plunder his prized possession: "YOU BASTARDS
/ GOT A LOT OF NERVE / TO CUT DOWN / MY ONLY
HICKORY TREE!"

At first, I was shocked by the language my father
used, but quickly my shock turned into pride and then
transformed into a kind of hero worship. He was standing
up to the bad guys, he was telling them off, he was in
the right, and he said exactly what he felt. He was right,

he knew it, and I knew it. He must have entertained the fantasy of sitting with his family at the table beside the kitchen window to look out on fox squirrels sitting in the branches of that young hickory tree chewing the hickory nuts they were having for breakfast while we ate our own breakfast of cereal or fried eggs and toast. Now those white hickory chips burned and glowed like hot coals in our minds.

Later, my mother planted near the site of the hickory-sapling massacre a shoot of the flowering almond tree that came from her great-grandparents' garden in Ireland, Indiana. Every spring it sent out its small and delicate pink flowers, and Mom would smile and hum as she watered her ancestral plant. She had gotten her shoot from her sister, my Aunt Frieda Hoffman, who had transplanted her offspring from the Ur-Schmitt garden.

As the house rose up from the foundation and took shape not far from the sugar maples and a white oak where we later had a patio and swing, the memory of that sacred hickory sapling receded in our memories. We often drove out from our Fifteenth Street house in Jasper to check on the progress the builders had made. First there was a hole, then there was a foundation, then there were room divisions visible in the "basement," then there was a stair that rose up to a first floor, then we could walk across what would be that first floor, then there was a staircase up to what would be the upstairs, and then there were rafters and planks laid out over what would be our boys' bedrooms on that level. One evening, after racing ahead of our parents, in a burst of untempered enthusiasm, my brother Eddie and I scampered up the stairs on hands, knees, and fingertips. When we got to the top, we stood up and tiptoed onto the loose planks, trying to keep our balance in the area where my bedroom would be. It felt as if we were tightrope walking.

All of a sudden, Eddie whooped as he lost his balance and slipped through a space between the loose planks. There was nothing I could do, except stand there, tottering myself, looking down. It was as though time and space froze. Our parents were still downstairs, looking up. Like Humpty Dumpty, little Ed hit what was to be the kitchen floor, but instead of splattering, he bounced up like a rubber ball and kept running until he was outside of what was becoming our new house. Then we all entered back into time, got into the car, and quietly drove home to East Fifteenth Street.

12

Moving into the New House

When we moved into our new house on Schroeder Avenue in March, grass seed had been scattered across the worked-over ground, and the lawn to be was covered with yellow straw. Across the rock road in front of the house was an open field owned by Holy Family Parish. The new sandstone Holy Family School, golden in the sunlight, was always in full view. We had to chug up a steep rock driveway to park the car in the garage. Dad hung a swing from a metal bar wedged between sugar maple and white oak trees and laid out a patio of flat fieldstones. On the hill of "the property," as we called it, there was always a breeze, even in the hottest, sultriest dog days of August. Swinging between those trees, with a good book propped on my lap, was to be suspended in time and place.

When we moved in, there was no house immediately on either side of us. Next to the driveway, extending down a slanted hill all the way to Justin Street, was a field of glorious shaggy weeds divided by a hedgerow along a shallow ditch, where we played cowboys and Indians all day long in the summer sun. We had bows and I made arrows out of a long weed with a pointed "conker" at the end. The biggest thrill was to sneak up on my brother Ed and plunk him in the butt with a long conker. We could roam through the rust-colored broomsedge and whoop to our hearts' content.

Behind the new house, but still on our property, the woods began. There were many sugar maples, but also a stand of sassafras, beneath which we built our sandbox; a sweet gum tree, whose star-shaped leaves flared red in the fall; and one black cherry tree, whose small dark fruit dropped down onto dry leaves in August. At the end of our property was a path that led across the wild-grass "alley" down into "the woods," another expanse where we ranged singly or in packs. My favorite blackberry patch was at the far edge of those woods, not far from my Uncle Fritz Krapf's house. When Fourth of July firecrackers popped, I knew it was time to pick blackberries. I put on a long-sleeve work shirt, which I wore also for hunting squirrels, dabbed my ankles with coal oil for protection against mosquitoes, put on a baseball cap, and picked blackberries by the gallon bucket. Mom baked sweet steaming cobblers and pies with the fruit I brought home, and whatever was left over I sold to the Jasper Bakery for a dollar a gallon. Near those blackberry brambles were some fallen trees and a stand of pokeweed in which quails loved to roost.

Sometimes I rambled farther down the rock road past the houses of Charlie Schuck and Orville Schroeder and turned left into a wild area that had been recently bulldozed. I tiptoed up to the edge of a mound of ashes where the developer had set fire to a mound of brambles and saplings after the bulldozer grew quiet. Poking out of the ashes I found mysterious green orbs, the unripe fruit of a mature black walnut tree that had been felled. I poked around with a stick in the wasteland ashes for other treasures and talismans.

ABOVE: *Christmas in the new house, 1953.* LEFT: *New house in the snow, woods behind.*

Or before I got to Schroeder's house, I could turn right at the Schucks and enter the little woods owned by Holy Family Parish. Near the corner of those woods was one of my favorite trees, a chestnut oak. Not far from that chestnut oak was an abundance of pawpaw trees, whose pulpy fruits (shaped like a soggy banana the width of a potato) I loved to pick up off the leafy ground and lug home heaped in my hands. Often near that corner of the woods, and in my favorite blackberry patch, coveys of quail would explode into flight in front of my feet, leaving my heart pounding beneath my T-shirt. Not far into those little woods, just up a slope, was the site of my most productive rabbit trap. Sometimes in late fall and winter I found a cottontail or an opossum inside the tripped box. I let the opossums go, but the rabbits I carried home thumping in a burlap bag. Sometimes the trap was untripped, sometimes it was tripped with nothing inside it but cold air, and I would follow my steaming breath back up the hill for a hot breakfast in the new house.

It was a pleasure to have my own bedroom for the first time. The single, southern-exposure window, the only one in the room, faced the maple trees just outside, the beginning of the woods on the right, and the garden on the left. One Christmas I got a Red Ryder BB gun as my gift. I brought it up to my room, opened the storm window so that I could shoot at a target of my choice, cocked the lever, which I unfortunately left open, thinking it would be "cool" to fire it as if from the back of a streaking horse, and pulled the trigger. The lever cracked against the back of my fingers and taught me a lesson I can still feel breaking across my right hand. One spring, when I was working on a gardening merit badge as part of my activities with Boy Scout Troop 185, I planted vegetable seeds in cutoff waxed milk cartons and placed them on the window ledge. Every day I watched the kohlrabi, lettuce, tomato, bean, and pea plants sprout and push their tendrils up through the soft loam that I watered faithfully. I measured my day by how much my plants had grown.

At night, I would open the copy of *The Collected Tales of Edgar Allen Poe* that my Uncle Arthur Krapf gave me. In the dark of night, alone in my room, where every sound from inside or outside the house seemed magnified to the breaking point, I read "The Tell-Tale Heart," "The Murders in the Rue Morgue," "The Masque of the Red Death," and my favorite, the nightmarish "The Pit and the Pendulum." As soon as I finished a story, I turned out the light, put my head under the pillow, and tried to fall asleep. Goblins, demons, and murderous madmen loomed beneath my eyelids. There were quite a few pits, and the same razor-sharp, glinting knife descended closer and closer to my flesh, in many of my dreams.

Summers I woke up to fresh southern breezes blowing through the screen and the sound of birdsong in the sugar maples just feet away. Cardinals, robins, sparrows, doves, and bluejays called and cajoled me into the new day.

13

The Twin Pin Oaks

The first fall after we moved into our new brick house on Schroeder Avenue, Dad arranged for us to transplant two pin oaks into the front lawn. I did not know it, but he had arranged with my Uncle Bill Schmitt, who operated Grassland Farms north of the Jasper city limits, to pick out and tag two good ones. Fall was the time to put in trees, Dad explained.

We drove out to Uncle Bill's farm in our dark-blue 1952 Dodge, parked it near the modern barn just off the road, then started up a pickup we drove along a lane to a point beyond where an old log barn still stood. With Uncle Bill's help, we dug out the two chosen saplings, wrapped and tied burlap bags around their earthbound roots, and heaved them onto the bed of the pickup.

The site where we dug up these healthy saplings was not far from the pond where my mother sometimes brought us to wade and splash on a hot summer's day. Once when I was little and Ed was a toddler, we were splashing near the sandy shore in the water of that pond, which we thought of as a lake. Mother and Aunt Lucy Schmitt, Uncle Bill's wife, were sitting on a blanket gabbing while Ed and I splashed and chattered in the muddy water not far away. All of a sudden Ed took off, his face down in the water, his feet kicking, as if he knew exactly where he was going, propelled like a self-powered miniature steamboat toward the deepest water. I don't remember if Mom saw what was happening, or I screamed, or Aunt Lucy pointed, but it was obvious that Ed was motoring away from the shore toward the middle of the pond. Mother, who did not know how to swim, exploded into action. She jumped into the water, her feet churning like a fullback hitting the line, took steps larger than legs the size of hers should have been able to take, and just at the point where her toes could still barely touch the bottom, grabbed little Ed by his ankle, pulling him to herself and holding him tight.

As we drove away with those pin oaks in the back of the borrowed pickup, however, the memory of that narrowly averted tragedy had faded like clouds on an overcast day when the sun bursts through and persists. Now we had a new house of our own, the grass was green, if a bit faded, from the waning of summer and the coming of fall, and Dad, with me sitting shotgun, drove back all the way south through town along Newton Street with our free living treasures from a relative's woods for all to see. The back of our new dream house was set into a woods, the front yard was bare, except for some bushes Dad planted, but now we would set things right. Every self-respecting front yard was incomplete without trees to provide shade for the house and shelter for birds.

We had already dug two holes in front of the house. Dad hosed them full of water, we lifted the saplings one at a time into a wheelbarrow, and we settled each into its hole. We then shoveled dirt around and on top of the balls and covered the dirt with mulch. Dad had already laid in some orange clay-tile pipes at an angle, through which we could water those saplings, which grew unbelievably large, beyond any size I could have then imagined.

In one photo that has survived, I am standing in front of one of the saplings in my Cubs Little League baseball uniform, probably during the summer after we transplanted those pin oaks. We did not notice it fully as it was happening, but every year those trees grew taller and taller, rising well above the roof of the house and spreading from side to side until their branches almost covered the entire front yard. Sparrows started to build nests in the branches and fox squirrels came out of the woods and climbed up the thickening trunks and sat on tree limbs waving their bushy tails back and forth.

Every year the saucer-shallow acorns fell to the lawn. Every year those leaves turned brown but clung to the branches long after all other leaves fell and were raked into piles and carried down the bank of the front lawn to be placed at the side of the rock road for pickup by a city

Below: In my Cubs Little League uniform, before pin oak and Holy Family School across the rock road. Inset: The pin oaks grew and the rye field became a softball diamond.

truck. Even well into the winter, the brown leaves clung and resisted the north winds that blew toward the front of the house and whipped against the double-pane picture window.

In time, the pin oak on the left facing the rock road began to grow taller and visibly outpaced its twin on the right. When we thought about it, we realized that the extraordinary growth spurt was caused by this pin oak's location near the cesspool beneath its roots. That did not, however, mean that the other pin oak was weaker. Once lightening struck its trunk and left a gash running up and down the side facing the house, but the smaller twin never gave up its hold on life.

Both of the trees were survivors, visible from afar to people driving along the Jasper-Ferdinand Road. The pin oaks we transplanted as saplings from Uncle Bill's farm stood as mighty signposts of our house and property and, in my mind, served as our guardians. As the saplings we carried across the new lawn in a wheelbarrow grew into their maturity, as the branches became larger, the trunks thicker, and the leaves fuller, I felt safer and safer in our house. The shade the pin oaks cast in the summer was protection against the heat of the sun and their leaves that cleaved into the winter offered silent proof that, despite all obstacles, life would continue.

14

The Rye Field

When we moved into the new house, the builders had sown grass seed and covered the ground with yellow straw all around the house. Not long after we settled in, the field across the rock road, which belonged to Holy Family Parish, was sewn with rye seed. As Lenny grew into a toddler who wanted to roam around the house and then the world, the rye seed germinated and grew into a beautiful blue-green expanse that rippled in the evening breezes. Through the picture window in our living room we observed the shifting surface of the rye field. One moment it would look blue, the next minute green, and then both blue and green at the same time. In time, a path began to take shape through the blue-green sea of rye and wound its way over to the corner of the new sandstone school building, where the temporary church was. For more than twenty-five years, this temporary church was located in what had been built as the school gymnasium.

One day Lenny disappeared. We panicked. Where could he be? I looked out through the picture window and noticed that the blue-green rye field now assumed the proportions and properties of an endless and dangerous ocean that could swallow anyone and anything. "Lenny!" we called as we ran around the neighborhood, looking for the little tyke. "Oh, Lenny, come back home!" I entered the rye field and followed that faint path, looking to my right, looking to my left, calling out, "Lenny, little Lenny, are you there?" Nothing. Only the sound of the breezes tousling the waves of the rye, the sound of my own voice getting lost in that great expanse of blue green.

Somehow Mom and I ended up together at the corner of the school, where the steps and entrance to the church were located. When we turned the corner onto Church Avenue, we saw Mr. Kreilein, father of Jack and Richie, walking toward us with Lenny holding his hand. Lenny had come toddling around the corner of the church and veered into his yard, right near where the cars swished by on the busy Jasper-Ferdinand Road. Lenny was saved and we walked back home on the side of that rye field, which had shrunk back to its normal proportions. The breezes that played on the blue-green surface regained their gentle touch and brushed the expanse with a beauty for the eye to savor and absorb.

The field where that rye grew and rustled took on different roles over the years. Before that rye was sown, there was a scene in which I was with my cousin Jim

Hoffman, who was my age, and my cousin Tony Krapf, who came through the woods behind the house to play. We were walking along the rock road that led from Schroeder Avenue to Holy Family School as a big bulldozer groaned away nearby. It was both thrilling and frightening to be so near that terrible earth-*fresser*. A machine that could devour earth could also devour boys! Somehow one of my shoes slipped off and tumbled down a ditch right into the loud machine's path. I was terrified; I had only one pair of shoes. I looked way up toward the driver, sitting in his cab behind a pair of goggles. He slammed on the brakes, let me climb down into the pit to pick up my shoe and climb back up out of that hole, and then stoked up the engine and started to roar away again, with putrid black smoke escaping in big bursts from the vertical exhaust pipe.

Another time Tony and I were playing in that field, where in the evenings the killdeer sounded their plaintive cry, "Kill deer! Kill deer!" Tony bent down and found a nest of nickels, dimes, and quarters. "Look!" he said, and I found another nest and stuffed the coins in my pocket. Tony looked for more, found none, but I discovered another nest of coins and stuffed my pockets with more treasure. Tony, who had made the great discovery, felt he should have gotten more of the loot.

After that field of rye was harvested, Father Othmar Schroeder, who loved to hunt, had a wooden shed built near the corner of the woods across the field from the house of Charlie and Laverne Schuck. In this shed, which

SCHOOL DAYS 1957-58
HOLY FAMILY

CLOCKWISE FROM BOTTOM: My father with his three sons in the new driveway; the three Krapf brothers on the back porch, Lenny on the right; and Lenny at Holy Family School.

we called "The Quail House," the priest raised quails that hatched from eggs he ordered from a company. Some of these fledglings he released to roam in the pokes and blackberry brambles that grew in rich profusion in a sunken area of the field next to the woods. From the front lawn, we could hear their "Bob *white*, Bob *white!*" song when the world was quiet.

Years later, the rye field became the softball field, with a wire fence separating left field from the corner of the woods, where a single chestnut oak and pawpaw trees grew. My father, who loved any ball game, sat on the front lawn in the evening, under a pin oak tree, on a folding chair, and watched the men and the women of the parish slug it out in their separate leagues. Many a foul ball came flying and rolling up the hill on the lawn. Those that he could reach, he tossed back, and those that Mother found later ended up in the garage or in the attic. Years after that, the grandchildren, my children and the children of my sister Mary Lou, played with them whenever we visited.

Lenny, who came to words slowly, never ran away from home again, though he later explored the wide world on the blue-green seas. One day he and I were standing on the side porch looking down the hill to Justin Street below, where we could see flaxen-haired Joie Gelhausen playing in his front yard. "Go-ie Gay-hahn-sen, Go-ie Gay-hahn-sen!" Lenny cried. "Gobby," which became a family favorite and regular part of our table discourse, was his earliest word for "gravy." "Please pass the gobby," we would say. One

Sunday morning we were seated in our regular pew, front right in the church-gymnasium, waiting for mass to begin, when neighbor Marcus Kuper came in by the side entrance at the front, holding his hat in his hand. "Poo Poo! Poo Poo!" little Lenny chanted, pointing toward his buddy. The parishioners giggled.

Most of the time, in my mind's eye, I still see the field across from the rock road as a blue-green expanse of rye. The path that begins at the edge of the rock road still bends in a gentle arc, through the rye, toward the corner of the school house. I still hear the cry of the killdeer and the song of the quail. I blink and men and then women are playing softball in the field and stoop down between pitches to pick up nickels, dimes, and quarters. All of a sudden, I hear the roar of a gigantic yellow caterpillar. Then it is quiet again, and Mr. Kreilein asks, with a sly grin, "Did you folks lose something? This little fella came to visit." Little Lenny stands next to him, looking up at us. He knows he's done wrong, but is glad he did it, and we give him a hug.

15

What She Said

As I have noted before, Mother grew up on a farm west of Ireland, Indiana. Her father died of consumption at the age of thirty-three, when the oldest of six children, my godfather Uncle Alfred Schmitt, was twelve. Mother was six. In her latter years, she told stories of the mandolin he played, his beautiful tenor, and the times he sang that German anthem of loss, "*Du, du liegst mir im Herzen,*" around the wood stove in the winter, and "*Stille Nacht, heilige Nacht*" in the church choir loft on Christmas Eve. He was a handsome man who wore his hair parted down the middle, as I have seen in his wedding picture of 1906. He bore a strong resemblance to the sons of my godfather, my cousins Frank, Pat, and Mike Schmitt.

To repeat a painful story I have already told, when Mother and her brothers and sisters were standing at their father's grave after the funeral mass, as the coffin was being lowered into the earth, their Grandmother Hoffman, in an act of cruelty that is hard to fathom, pointed down at the hole and said to them: "Look, your daddy's dead! You'll never see him again!" As Mom told me that story some seventy-five years later, she wept. Losing a father so early helped make her a devoted, caring mother; she took pains to point out that the way her grandmother treated her and her brothers and sisters when they lost their father so early made her determined "to be a good grandmother."

A good and devoted mother and grandmother she certainly was. When we moved into a solid new brick house in the Sunset Terrace Addition of Holy Family Parish outside the city limits of Jasper in March 1953, she had to be thrilled. The kitchen, the flower beds, and the vegetable garden were her domain. My cousins called her Aunt Dots, and later, after I moved away from home and married, I jokingly dubbed her Saint Dorothy of the Kitchen, a title that made her smile.

She canned, then later froze, enough vegetables from our family garden to feed a family of six for the entire year. In August we drove to the orchards in Washington, Indiana, and picked bushels of peaches that she and her sisters canned when we got back to Jasper. I supplied blackberries that I picked by gallons from the woods. She kept rhubarb plants growing on both the front and the back edge of the big vegetable garden, and it seemed that all summer there was a cherry, peach, rhubarb, blackberry, or apple pie or cobbler cooling on the kitchen window ledge. Often she made her own yellow egg noodles and dumplings and pounded them out on the kitchen table, where she left them to dry and we would snitch little squares to chew.

Almost always there was tapioca pudding—one of my favorites—cooking on the stove. Once she had a pot of tapioca cooking on the stove, forgot about it while doing a chore, and the pot "exploded," as she put it, sending tapioca all the way to the ceiling and dripping back down to the floor. She ran to the phone, called her sister, my Aunt Frieda Hoffman, and tried to clean up as much of the mess as she could before Frieda and Grandma Schmitt, who by then had moved from the farm to the same neighborhood in town, arrived by car. "I slipped and slid all over the floor, crying as I was trying to clean up," she told them when they walked into the kitchen. By then she was laughing, despite the burns on her shoulders, left exposed by the comfortable sun dress she was wearing.

In our earliest years in that house, we had all the space in the world to roam and play, and Mother encouraged us to have fun. Past our rock driveway, at the edge of our lot, was an ungraded hill gloriously wild with weeds and a creek, with saplings on either side, that ran down to the rock road at the bottom of the hill. Behind the house was the woods, recently logged, in which we and our cousins Tony and Janie Krapf, who lived in a house on the other side of the woods, played for hours at a time, especially by the creek, over which we built a makeshift log bridge.

Mother encouraged us to play hard and have as much fun as we could. If we were playing cowboys and Indians

Clockwise from Bottom, Left: Mother graduates from high school, 1930; Mother and her three sons, Christmas, 1953; and with her first son, winter, 1944.

in the field on the hill, she would call us and our playmates
to have some fresh lemonade she made from scratch. We
enjoyed the cool nectar while sitting on the swing between
the sugar maple and white oak trees in the backyard. If
we used the picnic table under the sweet gum tree as a
stagecoach, she brought us old shirts and vests to use as
costumes. She sometimes sat at the kitchen table and
looked out at our game playing through the window, on the
ledge of which she had just placed a cobbler or pie, while
she mended socks or patched our pants.

She wanted us to play as hard and long as we could
and then go to bed tired. She could be tender, she could
be gruff when one or all of us had been naughty and the
occasion demanded, and she could also be raucous and
earthy. If she saw that one of us had left our zipper open,
she would say, in a kind of cackle, "Barn door open, horse
might get out!" If a relative or neighbor was slow to make a
decision or return a borrowed item, she would finally blurt,
"Well, I wish she'd shit or get off the pot!" As she chased
the three of us boys up the stairs to bed at night, she would
goose us from behind and chortle, "*Gute Nacht, scheiß ins
Bett, bis kracht* (Good night, shit in bed till it cracks)!"

16

The Garden and the Strawberry Patch

After we bought half of the lot between our property and Charlie Schuck's, we planted a strawberry patch. At the edge of the woods, Dad put in some fruit trees (pear and cherry), probably to emulate Grandpa Benno Krapf's orchard at the home place in Saint Henry, but they never produced much fruit. After several failures, he became discouraged and settled for some successful boysenberry and raspberry bushes. Where the orchard and bushes and briars ended, the strawberry patch began, and in this quiet corner of the property a covey of quail sometimes congregated.

This strawberry patch was in addition to the large garden Mom and Dad had put in even before construction began on the house. For several years before the house was built and we moved in, we drove out from our house on East Fifteenth Street to tend the garden. It was perhaps sixty feet by ninety feet in size. In the front part, we had several kinds of tomatoes (Dad liked the big Beefsteak, Mom liked another variety that canned better), carrots, peas, green and yellow beans, spinach, carrots, kohlrabi, turnips, cabbage, brussels sprouts, beets, green peppers, radishes, onions, shallots (descended from Great-grandma Hoffman's garden), cucumbers, and rhubarb. The middle third was corn, and the back third was Dad's potato patch.

Thursday afternoon was Dad's afternoon off from the Krapf Insurance Agency, and from the spring through the end of summer he spent many hours on Thursday afternoon, weekends, and evenings in the garden. He put on a pair of old jeans, a faded blue work shirt from his days in the chair factory, and a strawhat and headed for the garden with a hoe and a sharpening stone. Though he was very short, I could always see his big strawhat, which he would lift off with one hand and with the other wipe the sweat from his forehead with a red bandanna he kept bunched up in his back pocket. He limped from row to row; removed weeds between tomato plants and rows of beans, peas, and corn; and paused to put a sharper edge on the hoe that he used with a deft touch and economy of movement. Around the sides of the garden, he felled weeds with a slow, smooth curl of the scythe.

In the office of the insurance agency and while visiting customers in homes in town or on farms out in the country, he was not always in control of events or his nerves, especially when it came to the settling of controversial claims and the collection of overdue premiums, but in the garden he was the lord of his domain. He kept the weeds hoed and the plants sprayed, and his special pet was the Concord grape arbor he had on the east and south sides of the garden. He fermented the grapes in crocks and, later, in an old whiskey barrel in the basement, making a bluish-red sweet wine that he loved to sip before meals and in the evening. "Makes a guy relax," he said with a grin, lifting his small wine glass to the light.

The potato patch was also his special preserve. He had a hand plow with which he heaped the mound rows, in which we placed the cut-up spuds from the supply we kept in the recreation room in the basement. It was fun to see the white flowers blossom; the vines turn yellow, brown, and wither; and then prepare to dig. As soon as the new or baby potatoes were ready, Mom would say to me, "Go out in the garden and dig up a bunch of potatoes. Here, fill this mixing bowl. And don't cut any in half, if you can help it!" I took special pride in not cutting any of the baby potatoes, but if I did, I would eat them raw, skin and all, after I hosed the cakelike dirt off the skins. She would boil the fresh, tender baby potatoes in their thin skins, cut them open, yellow them with butter, and serve them piping hot.

When the potatoes were ripe, we all worked together digging them up, cleaning them off, loading them into bushel baskets, hauling them on a wagon to the house, and laying them out in the recreation room on newspaper, where we could get them any day throughout the winter. We had parsleyed boiled potatoes, mashed potatoes, scalloped potatoes, stewed potatoes with spinach, German fries with onions made in bacon fat in the big iron skillet, and, sometimes on Sundays, golden-brown french fries that Mom made in the stove's deep fryer. We competed to be the one who got to shake the big brown paper bag (used to absorb some of the grease) containing the hot fries.

During the winter, we went to the basement for a Ball jar of green beans; tomatoes; turnip kraut or tomato juice, wonderful for beef barley vegetable soup; tomato or grape juice to drink; and peaches or grapes for dessert. Also in the fruit cellar were jars of grape and blackberry jelly and strawberry preserves, all just right for breakfast toast, pancakes, and waffles, and also for a jelly-and-butter-bread sandwich as afternoon snack. When we got a freezer for the basement, Mom froze peas, green beans, corn, peaches, and strawberries.

During summer days Mom worked in the garden— weeding, watering, and harvesting. Immediately behind the garage, Dad built a hotbed in which Mom grew Bibb and other varieties of lettuce and herbs. My most vivid memory of Mom working outside, however, has her in the strawberry patch on the west side of the house on a golden afternoon, after the sun had turned the corner around the back of the house on the south, and was shining brightly against the bricks on the western wall. In the evenings, we turned to the west, looked from our hill at the pinkish-red sky, and repeated what Mom had told us, "Look, the sky is red, Santa Claus is baking cookies!"

In this memory, the afternoon sun illuminates the straw between rows and plants in the strawberry patch. I am in the bathroom, looking out the open window, as a fresh breeze blows through the screen (in that house, if there was a breeze anywhere, we felt it because we were perched on a hill). Squinting into the radiance, I looked out the window and saw Mom, kneeling while wearing a strawhat and a pale blue sundress, picking strawberries. She was humming the happiest tune I ever heard, not one that I knew, but one she was making up as she went along, one strawberry after another, to express her feelings about this ripest of moments.

17

The Parish Picnic

During my youth in Jasper, Indiana, the whole
year revolved around the Holy Family Parish picnic.
Throughout the winter, our mothers met at various houses
for quilting parties. When the party was at our house, we
opened the living room, usually kept closed and unheated,
opened the heat ducts, and set up the quilt frame that
Mom had gotten from Grandma Schmitt. The ladies always
arrived early in the morning, happy, excited, and full of
energy. They stitched and talked, stitched and talked,
broke for the noon meal in the kitchen, exclaimed how
much they liked the beef barley with vegetable soup that
had been simmering all morning, returned to the living
room, stitched and talked, laughed, folded in some good
gossip for seasoning, broke in the middle of the afternoon
for coffee and sugar cookies, returned to the frame, and
stitched and talked until it was time to go before their
husbands got home from work. The quilts that they made

with their own hands in those rotating daylong sessions were proudly displayed on the lines strung around the Quilt Stand on the day of the picnic.

"Ladies and gentleman," the barker, a neighbor, would begin, "next we have this patchwork beauty. Just look at them colors! Wouldn't she look beautiful in your bedroom, Ottie and Leona? Step right up and get your tickets. You want three, Ma'am, very good, here comes Joe." And Joe, a Krempp Lumber Company carpenter apron strapped around his waist, the pockets stuffed with green bills, coins and tickets, would find the lady and sell her some tickets. When I progressed into the upper grades at Holy Family School, I was proud to be promoted to working in the Quilt Stand, and knew I spent a little too much time admiring the work of the neighborhood women fastened with wooden clothespins to the line the barker could pull toward him to bring up the next treasure of the moment. How could anyone not love quilts?

Early in the morning on the day of the picnic, a Sunday, several of us boys from the neighborhood met after early mass and tried to buy a pack of cigarettes, Lucky Strikes or Camels, to share for the day. The cost was a quarter. If we failed at that, if somebody's father happened to be in the vicinity and thwarted our plan, we would buy a little black plastic pipe at the novelty stand and rip off some dried corn silk from the vegetable garden at somebody's house. We worked leading ponies for a while—walking them in a circle with little kids on the saddles. When our shift

was over, we headed for the creek past the Blessingers'
house, puffed and coughed, and talked about who we were
going to marry. Of course we were all wrong in our boasts
and predictions. If we were smoking brown corn silk in a
miniature black plastic pipe, each time we sucked on the
stem, we inhaled a ball of fire, staggered back one step, and
stayed dizzy for a few seconds.

Around noon, when the sun was burning hot, it was
time to head for the cafeteria in the basement. The line
stretched out the side entrance and wound around the
corner of the school, but we were never daunted. We
made another round of the picnic grounds, checked out
the Paddle Stand, took a chance, watched the wheel circle
and hoped it would stop on one of our numbers, and saw
if we couldn't win some money to buy an extra Orange
Crush and a hamburger drowned in ketchup, or a hot dog
smothered in mustard, for an afternoon snack. We kept
an eye on the dinner line and made our move whenever it
dwindled.

The basement cafeteria, where large fans were set up,
was cooler than outside. Our parents always gave us enough
money for dinner and an "allowance" for spending at the
stands. Nobody had to worry about going hungry. After
grabbing a tray at the serving counter, we had to decide
whether we wanted fried chicken or roast beef, which came
with mashed potatoes and gravy, green beans or corn, cole
slaw, a buttered roll, and a drink. We held the fried chicken
in our hands and gobbled it with no shame whatsoever,

no matter how greasy our fingers. Paper napkins were free. We talked as loud and chewed as fast as we wanted, manners be damned! This was Picnic Day. We were on our own, and most parents looked the other way, as long as we did not disgrace ourself and the family name.

During the afternoon, we roamed from stand to stand, returned to the creek for another smoke, and began to plan our evening strategy. That girl that you liked, how were you going to meet her, and where? Somebody would carry a message, but you had to work out all the details or look like a fool, a coward, or both. When the shadows began to lengthen and the heat decreased, behind the tent at the Pony Ride Arena might be a good place to meet and sneak a kiss.

It was always nice to go home with a tingle on your lips, a belly that was full but not to the point of bursting, and a feeling that next year's picnic would be just as good. It was always easy to fall asleep on the night of the church picnic, the best day of the year, unless that grumble in your belly acted up again.

18

Meal Etiquette

Mother always cooked the main meal, which in the German fashion we ate at midday, in advance and let it cool until she could see Dad's car turn off Indiana 162, the Jasper-Ferdinand Road, opposite Conrad "Coonie" Blessinger's yellow brick house. Dad angled slowly toward and past Holy Family School, then through the playground on the road that dead-ended at Schroeder Avenue, and turned right. As soon as Mom saw him turn off the main road, through the windows in the sunroom, as we called it, she rushed to the kitchen and lit the burners so the food would be hot again when he pulled up the hilly driveway and parked in front of the garage.

We children would arrive from Holy Family School, take our places at the table just about the time Dad pulled up, and he would soon join us, but not before he pulled a colorful patterned apron out of a drawer and strapped it on as a kind of elongated bib. If he came home early or if it was a weekend and he was ready to eat before the food was finished, he took his place at the head of the table, apron strapped behind his back, sat in a bolt-upright position, and held his fork and knife. He was ready to go to work. There were not many times when Mom, who understood the situation, did not have everything ready by the time he took his place. Dad ate fast—faster than the rest of us—and when he was finished, he got up, took off his apron, and went into the sunroom to sit in the reclining rocker for a little snooze before he headed back to work. We knew better than to comment on his early departure, would not have dared leave early ourselves, but the father of a family had privileges that could not be challenged.

Before he returned to the insurance agency office, however, Dad always told Mom, in a mixture of German and some English, that she had cooked a good meal. I never saw him not eat with gusto everything she had cooked and served. When we were young, during the earliest years in the new house, Mom and Dad spoke a lot of Dubois Country Dutch at the table, but at the point when we were able to understand most of what they said, they stopped and reverted to mostly English.

The German I heard in those early years at our table, at family gatherings, and other social events, a mix of nineteenth-century German that included dialect words and phrases with some Hoosier English thrown in, was enough to give me a foundation in vocabulary and idiom so that I could express myself, albeit ironically and haltingly, with some of my classmates then and later. Of course, we were proudest, most highly regarded, if we could call one another curse words or insults in German: *Dummkopf, Scheisskopf, Scheissarsch, Arschloch, Schwanz, Alte Sau*. I always loved to sit in the company of my great-aunts and -uncles and listen to them klatsch in "Cherman" and chuckle. I absorbed more of their conversations than I realized then, as I discovered years later when I was finally able to take a semester in German on top of an overload of classes at Saint Joseph's College. I found I already knew a fair amount of vocabulary, although the priest-professor, himself of German descent, often corrected my pronunciation. To his educated ear, the sound of German coming off my country tongue sounded far from "high."

Mother was good at cooking such meats as round steak, roast beef, pork roast, rabbit, squirrel, or chicken, which she fried, then later preferred to bake, all prepared with thick, rich gravies that we poured over the meat, making ponds and lakes in our mashed potatoes. Always in the summer we had Bibb and other lettuces from the hot bed and fresh vegetables, including peas, green beans, butter beans, carrots, corn, broccoli, squash, beets, turnips, brussels sprouts, and onions. Of course there was a supply of potatoes to be dug right out of the garden in season or brought up from the basement recreation room. For dessert, Mom often served the tapioca pudding that was so often blubbing on the stove, or fresh pies, such as peach, apple, blackberry, or my favorite, rhubarb, which grew at the back of the garden. She also made apple, cherry, blackberry, and rhubarb dumplings that cooled on the windowsill next to the table.

One Easter we got a duckling as a gift. We named him Henry, and when the southern Indiana winter turned severe, we brought him into the basement and gave him shelter in some straw we scattered on the fruit-cellar floor. Henry slept below shelves holding Ball jars of canned green beans, beets, pickles, tomatoes, tomato juice, grapes, and peaches. One morning we came down to feed Henry, found an egg in the straw, and Henry became Henrietta. We could not keep Henrietta forever, and, being a practical farm girl still, Mom took action.

One day we sat down to Sunday dinner and looked at a feast. We had a bowl of creamy mashed potatoes, butter beans in a special white sauce, a boat of darker gravy, and a large platter of baked meat that looked something like chicken. After saying the "Bless us, oh Lord, and these thy gifts," we served ourselves plenty of everything and started to eat. All but Eddie, who was suspicious.

"What's this meat, Mom?" he asked.

"Oh it's good meat, Eddie, why don't you just go ahead and eat it?" Everyone was smacking his or her lips over the scrumptious feast, everyone but Ed.

"What's this meat, Mom?" he kept asking with a knowing little twist.

"Don't worry, Ed, it's so good, see how much everybody is enjoying their meat?" Ed, who knew all along what that meat was, refused to have any during the entire meal. He could not be fooled. He knew what happened to Henrietta.

19

Boy Scout Activities

After I was old enough to join Boy Scout Troop 185 of Holy Family Parish, I spent many hours, days, and weeks involved in Scout activities. Going to summer camp for a week at Camp Carnes near Jasper Lake (the name was later changed to Idlewild Lake) was a highlight of the year. I loved being away from home, sleeping out in the woods in a tent, and going swimming, canoeing, and hiking every day. It was fun to hear and tell stories (mostly imagined, mostly about girls), sit around a campfire singing songs ("She'll Be Comin' Around the Mountain When She Comes" and "My Gal's a Corker, She's a New Yorker"), and working on merit badges that had to do with outdoor life. I liked hearing taps at the end of day and reveille early in the morning, and, though the food could not compete with what we devoured at home, I even liked the experience of eating meals in common in the mess hall.

Climbing up the steep, root-bound trail to Eagles' Nest made us feel like we were paying for those sins we were afraid to confess, but that struggle to the top of the peak made us so blessedly tired even our German-Catholic guilt could not keep us awake in the thick dark, where eyes of invisible creatures glowed and their rustlings and cries rose to a crescendo. The shadows we saw on the roof and sides of our tent when a flashlight flickered on as somebody panicked were enough to call up emotions that stimulated a series of dreams, giving us more than enough material for the next impromptu storytelling session.

A spiral-bound blue cloth notebook in which I kept handwritten or typed records of all the work I did for merit badges on the way to receiving the Eagle Scout award preserves many of the details of my scouting experiences and some of my best childhood memories. For Gardening, I tested a hundred seeds of squash, grew lettuce in a hotbed, and started half a dozen vegetables in my bedroom from seed, dug potatoes and put them in bushel baskets, bunched onions, stored onions and potatoes in the basement, helped clean and can green beans, and put corn and peas in the deep freeze.

For Cooking, with my pal Jim Gutgsell I built a fireplace of clay and tile thirty-six by forty-eight inches at Camp Carnes. We mixed clay with water and set the tile into the clay, then we smeared the outside and the inside of the tile with clay, and after we had the tile laid and the mud smeared, we built a fire to dry out and bake the mud.

According to my notebook, the menu was as follows: "2 boxes Mrs. Grass Chicken Noodle Soup, .25; 4 pounds Hamburger, 1.56; 1 pound potatoes, .10; 2 cans corn, .24; 2 boxes pudding, .29; one half pound Cocoa, .53; 3 quarts milk, .71; Miscellaneous items, Bisquick, lard, butter, salt & pepper, paper cups and plates, .58; total of 4.56, about 45 cents per person."

For Fishing, I caught a channel cat on a rod and reel baited with earthworms on July 29, 1956, and on the same good day a crappie on a pole and line baited with meal worms. I caught a blue gill on a fly rod baited with black and white popper on August 2, 1956. "I cleaned these fish and we ate them at home," I indicated in my notebook. The kinds of bait I caught and used at different times were earthworms, catalpa worms, night crawlers, roaches, crickets, grasshoppers, minnows, and crawfish.

For Nature, I observed the following trees while hiking from my best friend Mickey Stenftenagel's house cross country to Camp Carnes three different times: beech, tulip poplar, different kinds of oaks, cedar, sumac, walnut, fir, maples, elm, ash, willow, hickory, persimmon, pawpaw, mulberry, star gum, birch, and wild cherry. I identified these flowers: daisies, dogwood, redbud, peach, and apple blossoms, as well as such grasses as sage (prairie), orchard, fescue, timothy red top, and clover. I spied a chipmunk, squirrel, groundhog, rabbit, opossum, skunk, raccoon, and deer and the following litany of birds: wren, robin, turtledove, martin, cardinal, bluebird, blue jay, indigo bunting, sparrow, mockingbird, killdeer, quail, redheaded woodpecker, starling, hummingbird, goldfinch, vesper sparrow, crow, kingfisher, whippoorwill, and white heron. As part of my training, I learned to recognize the songs of the quail, turtledove, owl, crow, cardinal, wren, mockingbird, catbird, blue jay, martin and sparrow. I put out two wren houses, which unfortunately had not yet been "inhabited" by the time I wrote my report for the board of review, but I also helped put up a martin box which had "ten pairs of martins and most of the other holes [were] inhabited by spatsies," and I helped my father put up one feeder. I trained myself to recognize the tracks of the squirrel, raccoon, skunk, opossum, rabbit, chipmunk, and fox, and I made plaster of Paris tracks of deer, opossum, and raccoon.

As my childhood dream was to become a forest ranger, for Forestry I was delighted to collect leaves of the following trees and tell what their wood could be used for: hickory, honey locust, hard maple, soft maple, mulberry, persimmon, sassafras, sycamore, tulip poplar, black walnut, willow, slippery elm, beech, sweet gum, and wild cherry. I also visited the Eckstein sawmill in Jasper with Francis Seibert and noted, "First of all, the logs are brought in within a radius of 50 miles of the mill." I then described the process of cleaning logs in the sawmill pond, stabbing them with a pike pole and having them carried up into the mill on a chute, stacking the logs on a pile, and the "kicker" lifting and turning them into the carriage. The "sawyer decides what width the logs will be cut. He signals this to the chief man on the carriage—called the setter—by finger signals. After the blocksetter receives the signal from the sawyer as to what thickness to cut, he in turn moves a lever which moves the log forward to this thickness. The other man on the carriage is called the head-dagger. He dags by means of a hook the logs on the carriage to keep them from rolling off. In a modern sawmill, however, the work of the last two men is done by the sawyer himself with buttons. In place of the block-setter is the electric setworks and in place of the head-dagger are air-dags. The carriage is now set to move the log into the saw, which is a ten-inch band. After the board comes from the edger, it is graded by the grader as to thickness, species, and grade. The boards are then taken out into the lumber yard to their respective piles to be air dried until ready for marking. Air drying means stacking the boards into piles so that air currents can carry out some of the moisture in the boards. These boards are left in piles for a period of ninety days or longer before being moved to various plants to be kiln-dried and then made into furniture."

For Hiking, between July 26 and August 25, 1956, I took, with a small group of scouts supervised by our pastor, Othmar Schroeder, five ten-mile hikes, for which I drew maps, and a twenty-mile hike on the Lincoln Trail on September 1. Here is a description of the first five-mile hike: "The first hike started at the Schnellville Road where it joints State Road 164 at Louis J. Eckstein's farm. We

Clockwise from Bottom, Left: Presenting the flag to Mayor Edwin Knies; receiving Eagle Scout award with Sylvester Kreilein, 1958; and in my Boy Scout uniform, 1956.

walked the blacktop road through Schnellville. We turned left at the mill over the road that leads to the Schnellville Lake. Then we turned left again and followed the road through the Claude Gramelspacher farm to the house of Silas Mehringer (Schroeder's brother-in-law). We started the hike at 2:00 o' clock and arrived at 5:00. It was a cloudy and pretty hot day." That was an especially enjoyable hike because Silas and Fronie Mehringer were like second parents to me. Silas was my mentor when it came to the art of squirrel hunting, and to end a hike at their house meant a delicious country meal and lots of attention and encouragement.

My most vivid scouting memory, however, is not recorded in the merit-badge notebook. One early spring a small group of scouts, including Jim Gutgsell and Dave "Blitz" Blessinger, went on a cross-country hike Friday after school to Camp Carnes, where we had the key to sleep in the mess hall. We walked along Giesler Road, then a rock road, until we came to a horseshoe turn in the road and left it for a recently plowed field that was deeply furrowed. Soon we were all shouting in glee as we saw an old snapping turtle hunkered down in a furrow. "Turtle soup, turtle soup, turtle soup!" we chanted. What a great opportunity this would be to please our mothers and bring home the surprise goods for fresh turtle soup, a specialty then at the popular annual parish picnics. There was no way, however, that we could lug that tough old snapper all the way to Camp Carnes and back home. He was too

heavy to carry, if we chopped off his head with a hatchet
the meat would not keep until we got back, and so we
decided to outwit that stupid old critter. We put our crafty
young heads together, turned that snapper upside down in
the furrow, and put a heavy rock on his belly plate. That
would surely keep him there until we returned late the next
afternoon.

We hiked back the next morning after a sleepless night
of jabbering in the dark and shivering with the cold and in
fear because we had found monumental footsteps beneath
the mess hall floor, and were sure we would be attacked by
the Abominable Snowman (though winter was over) the
moment we fell asleep. We made all sorts of promises to
the Virgin Mary to make novenas and say countless rosaries
if we were saved. When we came to our plowed field, we
picked up the pace so that we could fetch our treat of turtle
meat for our mothers and be praised for our cleverness
and memorialized in legend. Of course, that wily, patient
old turtle had found a way to turn himself over and crawl
back to safety in the nearest creek. We arrived home
with no fixin's for turtle soup, but with more than enough
ingredients to concoct some spicy stories.

20

Sunday Morning Baseball

In the early years of the parish, there was no Saturday evening mass at Holy Family Church, and there were only two Sunday morning masses, at 6:30 a.m. and 8:30 a.m. After everybody finished breakfast, the guys in the neighborhood, and some from beyond, gathered for the weekly Sunday morning baseball game on the parish property.

Two of the older guys, say Jack Kreilein and Junie Blessinger, who was so good at shooting squirrels that he started to fire from the hip, without aiming, to avoid boredom, served as captains and flipped a bat in the air, alternately placing their closed fists up to the rim at the base of the bat, and whoever got in the last full hand got first pick. Other players included Ken and Dave "Blitz" Blessinger, with whom I later hauled hay, and whose younger brother Jackie drowned in the hole that was to be the basement for a new church that was never built;

their cousins Jim and tough, spring-legged Charlie "Chas" Blessinger, both of whom drowned in the Patoka River one summer Sunday, sending the neighborhood into a paroxysm of shock and grief; tall Larry Loechte, who much later died of a brain tumor; Dan "Buddy" Friedman, an Eagle Scout and standout running back in high school; the Stenftenagel brothers, "Dimp" (Ron), who died in a car crash right in front of his house after a high school football game, and Larry, fleet-footed Larry Dick; Kent and Ronnie Kuntz; my best friend, Mick Stenftenagel, an outstanding athlete in high school and college who married my beloved cousin Mary Ellen Betz, whose brother Jim was later a football teammate of mine and attended Saint Joseph's College with me; and sometimes Charlie Seng and others.

Mick and I were among the younger players when this Sunday-morning tradition began. The older guys arrived fast on their bikes, locked their brakes, skidded to a dramatic stop, hopped off their bikes, and started to play pitch and catch with one another to warm up. But not for long. It was as though everybody knew when the game must start and all the players arrived almost at the same time, ready to slug away. I don't remember anybody ever wearing a shirt for those Sunday morning games, and many guys did not wear shoes. Most of us went barefoot throughout the summer, broke our feet in, as we said, until the bottoms were so tough we could walk down Schroeder Avenue, a rock road, without flinching, or even walk across a stretch of hot tar without letting anyone see a tear slide out of the corner of an eye.

The baseball diamond was set up with home plate not far from two basketball goals, with black cinders as the floor, where in the late fall and winter I shot hoops pretending I was Oscar Robertson. Some of the time I pitched, sometimes I played first, sometimes I played third, but most of the time I played outfield, which gave me a lot of chances to roam because the big guys could really slam that ball. Centerfield was bounded by the rock road leading from the church to Schroeder Avenue, which ran in front of our house. If somebody lifted the ball on a fly over that road, he almost inevitably had a home run, for no matter how fast the fielder chased the ball down and how hard and straight he fired it in, the big guys could run the bases really fast. Larry Dick was especially swift. "Ooh la la!" he would say as he hit one hard and took off. Leftie Junie Blessinger, the squirrel hunter deluxe, swung from the heels at every pitch and cursed when he did not connect. Buddy Friedman hit the ball with a crack that had its own distinct sound. I was a line-drive hitter, with a decent ability to hit the ball where the fielders weren't, but my pal Mick had an explosive energy in his bat, even at a young age. If I had a talent that distinguished me, it was probably being able to run down long flies in the outfield and make catches that robbed the big guys of home runs. Robbing them with a flash of the leather gave you a kind of distinction and might lead to being chosen early by one of the captains the next time around.

Some of the guys were patronizing to younger players, and some, like Jack Kreilein and Kenny Blessinger, who became business partners operating a Sinclair gasoline station near the Patoka River, and Buddy Friedman, were kind and encouraging. A pat on the back after a good play in the field or a good at bat went a long way toward making you play even better than you had played in the previous inning or the last game. As some of the guys got older and moved on to high school, thus too big and old for the game, we younger guys came into our own and took positions of respect.

The same group of elders who dominated these games at first also divided into teams that had dangerous BB-gun fights inside and on the outskirts of local woods. I never joined these fights, which held no appeal. Why risk having your eye put out just to prove you can be a man? Playing hard and well in a baseball game that followed established rules, even if they were sometimes bent, was one thing. Trying to hit someone with a BB, maybe in the eye, was not an acceptable thing to do for someone who understood that if you hunted, you *never* pointed any kind of gun at any human being, even your worst enemy. Some games are worth putting your heart into, I knew then, but others are not worth even playing. Using a bat to hit someone over the head, even in a fit of temper, was wrong. Using a gun, even one that fired only BB's, to shoot at another human being, even one you detested because he made fun of you, was shameful.

That Holy Family playground where we played those Sunday morning baseball games was the scene of many feats and some disappointments. I remember going back to grade school in September in seventh and eighth grade, standing on that field and thinking, not about baseball, but about the future. I had the sense that I must do something special, must find the thing that I was called to do. Yes, I loved sports, but I did not sense that my future lay there. I loved scouting, but I knew that scouting was an apprenticeship that would, if it ended properly, lead to accomplishments in whatever field I chose as a career. Many of the adult leaders in Troop 185 of Holy Family Parish implied or stated outright that perhaps I should go to the seminary at Saint Meinrad, the local Benedictine Archabbey, and become a priest. Although I respected the religious dedication of my older friends, such as Jim Blessinger, who became a priest, and Mark Buechlein, who became a Benedictine monk, Bishop of Memphis, and Archbishop of Indianapolis, I knew that the seminary was not for me.

There was *something* I would and should do to make use of whatever talents were mine, but I did not know at the time what those talents were. Standing on that playground where we played those epic Sunday morning baseball games, I did have a sense of what my mission was *not*. Only after I laid down the bat, which I loved to hold, polish, and swing with a flick of the wrists, only after I picked up the pen, many years later, after I had moved far away from Jasper, only then did I come into the fullness of my powers. To write about my ties to the place where my family had lived for a hundred years before I was born was my mission: to show how the past lives in the present and that those who help make us into the individuals we become, live on in us. To celebrate and explore the lives of obscure people few could or would care to write about, was a mission that fulfilled the sense of purpose I intuited but could not envision while standing on that baseball diamond laid out on the playground across the street from the house in which I grew up. I would try to show that a baseball diamond on a school playground in a small town in the hills of southern Indiana could stand for the universe. I would have to move far away from Jasper, however, to discover that, if I wrote about it well, my hometown could stand for any place, and many people, in the world.

21

The Little Saint Joseph's Church

Wherever you stood in Jasper, Indiana, when I was a child, you could see the tower of Saint Joseph Church. Under the direction of their pastor, the Reverend Fidelis Maute, OSB, parishioners built the Romanesque church of sandstone quarried from the Eckert farm across the Patoka River and hauled to the construction site on sleds pulled by a team of oxen. The walls are four to six feet thick, the columns—poplar trees cut from local forests—are sixty-seven feet tall, the building is approximately eighty-three by 193 feet, and the steeple, completed after the construction period of 1867 to 1880, with plastering and other interior work finally completed in 1888, towers 235 feet tall. It is a magnificent structure, a monument to the spirit and communal pride of the German-Catholic people who built it.

I received my First Communion in Saint Joseph's Church and was confirmed there. Every Sunday I went to mass there, until we moved to Holy Family Parish, outside the town limits, in 1953. The first time I ever went to mass on my own, I walked there by myself from our house at 415 East Fifteenth Street, taking care when I crossed busy Newton Street, also known as U.S. 231. It was Thanksgiving weekend. I wanted to go to church and Mother gave me permission to go by myself. When I arrived in the church, which I entered from the side entrance on the south, I noticed that there were an awful lot of people already in the church, even though it was early. I found a seat, and when everyone rose and walked in succession to the communion rail, I followed. I did not want to be left out of anything and wanted to be able to report that I had done everything I was supposed to. Shortly after I returned to my pew, everyone rose in unison and walked out of the church, so I followed them again and retraced my steps up Newton Street, turned right on Fifteenth Street, and came into the house.

"What, you're back already!" my mother said. "What happened?"

After I explained, she chuckled and said, "It's okay, but all you did was go to communion during the early mass and left when that mass was over. You didn't go to a whole mass. But don't worry, it's okay." She laughed, phoned her sister Frieda, told her what had happened, and the story made the family and neighborhood rounds.

My father always loved Saint Joseph's Church. During the Great Depression, he had moved to Jasper from the village of Saint Henry, where he was born, to work at the Jasper Chair Company. He roomed with his sister, my godmother, Aunt Flora, and her husband, Uncle Mike Schwinghamer. Dad loved to tell stories about Father Basil Heusler, a Benedictine priest who was quite a character. Basil, who enjoyed assuming his position of power high in a wooden pulpit at the church, had a reputation as an imposing preacher, but sometimes he came down to earth fast.

One Sunday, according to my father, Father Basil was preaching away and saw a woman look at her watch. Peering right at her, he said in German, "Hey, *you* down there, you don't have to look at your watch. If you got a roast in the oven, it's gonna burn for sure. I ain't nearly done talkin'!"

As Dad explained to me, once upon a time Father Basil saw a parishioner and friend named Eckerle coming down the walk toward the church. "Hey, Eckerle," he asked, "you got a shotgun?"

"Ja, sure, what you wanna do with it, Father?"

The good pastor answered: "The doves are shittin' all over my Saint Joseph!"

My father's love of the church moved him to make a replica of it that stood every year under the Christmas tree. We placed it near the stall with the Nativity scene, a wooden well, with winch, that he also made, and a miniature log cabin my Great-uncle Alphonse Krapf had given me because I always admired it and played with it

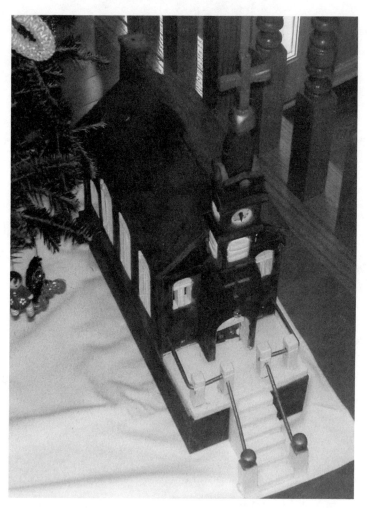

Built in the 1950s after we moved to Holy Family Parish, the little church has been relocated in the twenty-first century to downtown Indianapolis.

when we visited him and Aunt Lizzie at their house on Jackson Street. Like Dad, they had moved into town from Saint Henry and opened and operated the O. K. Grocery down the street from their house.

I remember Dad working painstakingly at his workbench, nights and weekends, to make his wooden church an accurate model of the great pioneer sandstone building that was the center of life in Jasper. He would measure and figure, draw lines, saw, chisel, rasp, whittle, figure some more, sand, and, when he was finally satisfied he had gotten it right, step back and admire his work. The slanted overhanging roof and sides were plywood, stained walnut brown. He cut out rectangular openings on the sides for windows, then inserted as crosspieces cut strips of plywood, which he attached, and glued colored cellophane paper on the inside of the crosspieces and walls to replicate the beautiful stained glass in the original. The steeple he cut out of a separate piece of wood, glued to the back side of the church, added trim, and attached a separate miniature cross, rounded and smooth to the touch, at the top. He painted the elevated cross a metallic gold. On each of the four sides of the tower, he hand drilled with a bit a slightly recessed circle, wrote in each with a pencil in Roman numerals the twelve hours, and attached with screws, in the center, metallic hands he cut out.

Over the main entrance to the church, my father screwed in a flashlight bulb so that no Saint Joseph parishioner might stumble. He made one architectural change: whereas the side entrance on the south of the actual church has stone steps leading up to it, Dad put his wooden steps, with railing, at the main entrance on the south. Therefore, we had to elevate the little Saint Joseph's Church on a shoebox covered with a sheet (snow) so that the steps could hang over the box and below the floor of the church. These steps, painted white, were wooden, and Dad also made wooden posts through which he drilled holes so that the thick wire railings could be pulled. He painted these railings gold—the same metallic gold he used on the cross perched atop the steeple.

After we moved to Holy Family Parish, where mass was held in the school gymnasium because there was no church, we had our own Saint Joseph's Church beneath the Christmas tree. Most years Mother flocked our tree, which Dad, Ed, and I picked out and cut on Uncle Cornelius Krapf's farm on the Celestine Road. She decorated the snow-white Scotch pine with green, blue, and pink glass ornaments she collected, as well as tinsel and strings of colored lights. We sat on the sofa in the living room, kept closed and unheated most of the year, looked at the tree, ate the glazed cookies she baked and the chocolate candies she made, and admired the little Saint Joseph's Church. I learned rather early, from example, that the best prayer you can say, the highest praise you can give, the best legacy you can pass on, is what you make, of your own spirit, with hands that transfer love.

22

The Living Room in Winter

In the winter, Mom and Dad closed the vents in the living room and shut the two doors. Since we did not need the space for our daily lives in winter, to have heated the room would therefore have been wasteful. There were, however, three exceptions. I was allowed to practice my trombone in the unheated room after supper. When it was Mom's turn to have the quilting bee at our house, the room was opened and heated for the day. When the Christmas season arrived, we opened the doors and the vents and gathered in the room to sit and look at the Christmas tree, which we placed before the picture window, and daydreamed about the gifts we would receive.

Practicing the trombone in an unheated room in the winter after supper while others were doing dishes was no enticement to a musical career! I put on a Perry Como cardigan sweater, buttoned it up, tried to warm up the cold mouthpiece with my hands so that my lips did not have to

suffer, and tooted and "slid" my way through several songs
in the little book I placed on a collapsible metal stand.
Sitting there shivering, I played "When the Saints Come
Marching In," "Anchors Away," "Over the Rainbow," and
my favorite, "Beautiful, Beautiful Brown Eyes," which
Mother loved to sing. To be honest, I was glad when it was
time to take apart my Conn trombone, pack it in its case,
close the doors behind me, and walk back into the warmth
of the kitchen.

One of the best aspects of the annual Holy Family
Picnic, which I have described in another chapter, was the
quilt stand. All the quilts raffled on this glorious Sunday in
high summer were made by the women of the parish, who
took turns quilting in one another's house. Mom inherited
her mother's quilt frame, which we kept in the attic and
brought out when it was her turn to host. Then we opened
the living room doors, opened the vents, and let the oil
burner cook until the room warmed enough so that the
ladies' fingers could be nimble. There was plenty of light
in the eyes of those parish women when I walked into the
room and they looked up from their quilting.

The ladies always made a fuss over my little sister Mary
Lou, who came late into our family, years after my first
sister, Marilyn, had been stillborn. For a boy not to have a
sister is to live with a part of himself incomplete, and for
a family with three boys to be blessed with a sister as the
last child "to come into the world," as the Germans say,
lifts that family to a new and welcome level of completion.

The quilters, all mothers, of course understood that, shared in Mom's belated joy, and showered their affection on little Mary Lou. What better way to spend a winter day for an only daughter than in a houseful of women quilting in companionship, incessant conversation and laughter making her mother smile and hum? To hear her name called over and over with such affection when Mary Lou was so young was to hear a song whose melody and rhythms stayed with her forever. Toots, a common name for sisters and daughters in Jasper, or Tootie, was what my Dad called Mary Lou, whom I later dubbed Mary Blue.

The highlight of every year was the Christmas season, which was centered in the living room. We roamed in and out of the room to savor the seasonal delights, sometimes plopping on the floor or on the couch and staring at the decorated tree and the vital scene below, a kind of miniature village that reflected life in Jasper and life in the New Testament, magically combined. The Jasper prop was the wooden miniature Saint Joseph's Church that Dad built at his workbench in the basement and occupied a prominent location under the tree. Dad also built a small, roofed well with a metal bucket that could be lowered by turning a handle. The biggest structure to rest beneath the tree was a wooden stable with a loft, in which Mom placed statues of the Holy Family, shepherds, and strands of yellow straw.

For years, we picked and cut our own Christmas tree on the farm owned by Uncle Cornelius Krapf, with

whom Dad operated the Krapf Insurance Agency. This
farm, along the Celestine Road, was mainly uncultivated
land with a woods that Uncle Cornelius let grow wild. He
planted the rolling land near the road with an abundance
of small Scotch pines that eventually grew to be the right
size for Christmas trees. Dad, Ed, and I packed a saw and
hatchet in the trunk, drove to the site, hiked around the
hills, and looked for just the right tree as our breath puffed
white in the cold crisp air. After we made our selection,
Dad started sawing, the smell of cedar or pine sap rose in
our nostrils, and the three of us carried the cut tree back to
the car, nestled it into the trunk, and tied the lid shut with
shaggy binder twine.

Mom enjoyed decorating the tree. She strung it with
beaded popcorn and colored lights and hung it with tinsel
and glass ornaments that were hand painted. Dad put "The
Dance of the Sugar Plum Fairies" from the *Nutcracker
Suite* on the stereo, and we kids helped place and hang the
boxes of ornaments we carried down from the freezing cold
attic.

Not long before Christmas, Mom began baking cookies
and making candies that she laid out on the long living
room end table we placed against a wall, for this season
only. She baked crescent and oatmeal and raisin cookies,
but what she baked the most of were sugar cookies, which
she covered with red and green sprinkles. She had a press
that allowed her to cut the dough in the shape of small
stars, pinwheels, Christmas trees, hearts, moons, and

reindeer, as well as the traditional bigger round shapes. Grandma Schmitt had always baked many dozens of sugar cookies for her great-grandchildren (we grandchildren usually got silver dollars), but when she could no longer handle all the baking by herself, Mom, Mary Lou, Aunt Frieda Hoffman, and her daughter Sara gathered together with Grandma to bake Christmas cookies all day long.

Ed and Len in front of the tree and the crèche in the stable, 1953.

Mom also made white divinity fudge; coconut butter pinwheel candy that consisted of a layer of mashed potatoes and another of peanut butter, along with salt, sifted powdered sugar, and vanilla; truffles, which were melted chocolate laid out on waxed paper and rolled in coconut; and my favorite, bourbon balls, which smelled and tasted of whiskey. When she made these bourbon balls, Mom secured them in tins, which she hid under her and Dad's bed for the coolness gathered there, and for safekeeping. We knew we were not allowed to pilfer the sacred bourbon balls until she laid them out on that end table with the other cookies and candies, next to the fruit baskets and fruit cakes that arrived as gifts from relatives.

Another essential part of Christmas was the tangerines Mom kept in the unheated living room closet next to the front door that faced north. When you peeled one of these cold tangerines, you could smell the flavor bursting through. Sometimes during the Christmas season I would get up early, before anyone in the family, to make a raid of some bourbon balls and a tangerine before breakfast started. Christmas, which came only once a year, was not a time to worry about what might happen to your belly if you ate too much of the wrong kind of thing at the wrong time of day or night.

23

The Workbench

Dad's wooden-plank workbench was in the furnace room in the basement, facing the south wall and a small window whose glass I broke more than once playing pitch and catch with Ed. The times I broke that small pane, through which some light did leak onto the workbench, I had to walk to Messmer Lumber Company with the right measurements, buy a new pane of glass (the second time, with my own funds), put it in place, and putty it. Above the wooden surface of the bench was an electric light with a metal saucer type of fixture that focused light on the area where Dad worked at night after he came home from selling insurance. To the right was the oil furnace, which kicked in with a blast in the winter and kept the room rather snug.

Out of plywood he stained dark brown, Dad built and hung on the concrete wall a tool case with doors that had shelves that opened on hinges and could be locked with a clasp. Inside this plywood case, hung on the back panel or placed neatly on the door shelves, were saws and hacksaws, wrenches (some adjustable), chisels, hammers and mallets, screwdrivers, small and large planes, a hand drill with many bits, pliers, shears, rasps, files, levels, squares, an awl, wooden and metal yardsticks, sandstones for sharpening small knives, various kinds and sizes of nails and screws in small jars, an assortment of sandpapers, some knives and putty knives, and carpenter's pencils. On the right-hand side of the bench was a strong vice; on the left was a small round knife-sharpening stone that was turned with a handle. When Dad worked with the tools housed in his case, they always stayed oiled, shiny, and in place. Most of the time, his eldest son put them back where they belonged, but when he didn't, a frown was enough to freeze him into obedience at the next opportunity to prove himself.

Dad loved to build bird boxes at his basement workbench. He liked to build bluebird boxes and "Chonny wren" boxes, as he called them, but his specialty was building the multitiered, many-holed deluxe houses for the martins he so loved, described in another chapter. When he started a martin box, we knew it was a project that would occupy him many week nights and weekends. He liked to "figure," as he called it, and make sketches of what he would build. I liked to assist him, hold boards for him as he sawed, sweep up sawdust, and fetch just the right tool he needed for the detail he was working on. "You have to have the right tools," he would say, "to get the job done."

Even at a young age I understood that this working with wood was a way of holding onto to the work he did in a chair factory for twenty-five years, before he joined the Krapf Insurance Agency. I also sensed, from the stories he told, that making these bird boxes and other objects was a way of carrying on the tradition of working with wood that his father, Benno Krapf, did with his steam-engine sawmill in and around the village of Saint Henry, near the southern border of Dubois County. I enjoyed watching Dad glue, screw, and nail pieces of sawed wood together into shapes that eventually became a satisfying whole. I especially enjoyed watching him turn a screw in real tight with the long Yankee screwdriver that allowed him to apply just the right amount of pressure. He always gave a loud sigh of satisfaction when he gave a screw its last turn or a beer its last sip.

He showed me how to build my first rabbit traps at that workbench. I started with wooden boxes we got from the hardware store, and he showed me how to make a trapdoor in the top, through which I would peer to see, when the trap was tripped, if a rabbit was huddling inside or if all the box held was cold air. He also advised me on how to build the fancier pyramid style of trap that the older guys in the parish boasted of using. These I built of a series of squares that got smaller and smaller and culminated in a hinged trapdoor at the top. Even from a distance I could see if I had a rabbit, a possum, or nothing when the trap was tripped. Being able to see the results so far in advance did relieve some tension, but it also reduced the thrill of finding out only when I opened the trapdoor whether I would bring home a rabbit for my mother to fry and then bake with onions until it was tender.

One of my favorite objects that my father made— something I eventually chose as part of my inheritance— was a little box with two compartments he made out of three-quarter-inch plywood. One of my jobs each week was to polish the shoes of everyone in the family, usually on Saturday so that they shined for church on Sunday. On one side of the box, which had a raised and arched piece of higher plywood as a divider culminating in a handle he had smoothed with sandpaper, I kept liquid and wax polish of various colors. On the other side, I placed the brushes and cloths for applying and buffing. Some of the shoes were brown, some oxblood, some black, and some, mother's and Mary Lou's, were white. In the early part of my apprenticeship as a shoe polisher, I used liquid polish, but I knew you could never do a satisfactory job applying that gook to cover up the scuffs, which always returned at the first touch of shoe with anything solid. Not until I graduated to the rank of applying liquid wax did I begin to take pride in my work and feel that I had lived up to the honor of holding that little shoe-polishing case my father built with the tools he kept, with pride, in the case he built of wood, with his own hands.

24

Going for the Long Ball

The discolored, scruffy looking "Wilson made in U.S.A. horsehide cover " baseball is covered with signatures in faded blue ink. Two names are the managers of the 1956 Little League All Stars, Jasper, Indiana: Vic "Peewee" Bohnert and Carl Seng. The others, my teammates, include: Mike "Mick" Stenftenagel, Chuck Berger, Allen Henke, Jim Klein, Bill Weikert, Mike Bohnert, Bob Merder, Dwight Ludwig, Cyril Mehringer, Ken Kreilein, Bob Waddel, Jerry Rees, Bill Schuler, and Jack McCune.

I remember what it was like, in my childhood, to lie awake at night and wonder why I couldn't make more of myself. Each year of grade school began with a resolution to improve myself. I could not have put it in such moral terms then, but I often resolved at the beginning of a new school year to make myself a better person—to rid myself of those imperfections that, because of the rigidity of the German-Catholic environment of my childhood, made me feel like a bad person. I felt guilty and sensed that my relationships with my classmates would improve if only I could rid myself of these personal faults.

My most vivid memory of lying awake takes me back to the summer of 1956. At the age of twelve, and therefore in my last season, I was a member of the Cubs Little League baseball team. I could not sleep that night because I had not yet hit a home run. Singles, doubles, triples, yes; but home runs, no. That night I had rapped out two line-drive singles. Not a bad night for a good spray hitter, but it weighed heavily upon me that in the eyes of my teammates and friends on opposing teams, one did not achieve stature and ultimate respect unless one hit home runs.

It came as a shock when, in my last year of Little League, the year when I was supposed to have the strength and power to pound the ball over the fence, my manager, a respected authority figure in my eyes, confronted me with my apparent inability to hit the long ball. I had, after all, been on the All-Star team the year before.

"I have to admit," the manager, a friend of my father, said to me in the presence of my younger brother Ed, a teammate, before a game, "that I thought you were going to hit home runs for us this year. I'm disappointed." I looked up and saw several teammates nodding.

If I had not been aware of this expectation—my teammates had, in the cruel way that young friends sometimes convey their disapproval, often hinted that I was not measuring up—I would not have been so crushed.

ABOVE: *Our father and his Little*
League baseball team, 1955, with
Ed and Len on the minor league
Yankees. RIGHT: *Batting practice in*
my Cubs uniform, 1955.

I wanted to fulfill everyone's expectations and knew that I had not.

That was why I lay awake that night, wondering what I was doing wrong. Why had I disappointed my teammates and manager? Why was I not able to equal the hitting feats of others who, as everyone agreed, had no more talent than I? I took pride in my defense in the infield and outfield, was proud to be able to contribute as a pitcher, was proud that I could hit line drives to all fields, but I was ashamed that I could not lift the ball over the fences and circle the bases like others my age were doing and receive applause and approval as I stepped on home plate.

In the All-Star game that summer, against another team from somewhere in southern Indiana, I won a measure of respect, but it was something of an accident that I "proved" I was the guy who could hit the long ball. My first two times up, I hit a solid single and a triple, and the third time around I hit one of the hardest balls I ever hit, a screaming line drive that the second baseman could not handle. He knocked it down, but was given an error on the play. So I was two for three when I stepped up the fourth time, thinking I should have been three for three.

I don't remember the count, but let's say it was a strike and two balls. The pitcher threw a high and outside fastball, clearly out of the strike zone. I was seeing the ball so well, as big leaguers like to say, that I didn't know if I should swing, even though the ball was clearly out of the strike zone. As a hitter, I loved the ball high and outside.

At the last minute, as a reflex action, I took a kind of half swing. I merely flexed my wrist in an uppercut at the last minute and watched the ball arch high and gracefully over the green picket fence in the right field corner. My neighbor Allen Sternberg, who happened to be standing right there behind the fence, later told Ed, at the time seated in the stands, that the ball just barely cleared the fence.

Perhaps because I had been trying for so long to hit the long ball and finally succeeded by accident, I was embarrassed when my All-Star teammates mobbed me at home plate and welcomed me into the club of guys who hit for real power. Next day the headline on the sports page of the *Jasper Herald*, the local daily, proclaimed that I had led the team in hitting and had slugged a home run, the only one I ever hit even though I continued to play baseball through high school. According to the coach, I could handle the curve better than any of my teammates, I was skilled at hitting the ball where it was pitched to all fields, and I especially loved to take the ball to the opposite field. But that unexpected, gratuitous moment of glory in an All-Star game in my last year of Little League baseball cured me forever of the itch to go for the long ball.

25

The Night the Game Was Called

From the time that I was five or six, every Sunday night I would go with my dad to the Jasper Reds game at Recreation Field. At the time, they played in the IK (Indiana Kentucky) League and were considered a semipro team. This was baseball with a Hoosier German accent.

Several of the players, Hoffmans, were relatives on my mother's side of the family They included Brute, first the catcher, later the manager; Eddie, the catcher who replaced Brute, a leftie with a wide-open stance; Bumps, the leftie first baseman pull hitter who dumped them into the old swimming pool beyond and below the chain-link fence in right field; and also Chick Alles, the power-hitting outfielder who married Eddie and Bumps's sister Annie and later served as Jasper's mayor.

Other colorful players that stand out in memory are Rags Burger, the manager who always puffed on or chewed a cigar; Rocky Renneisen at third; and Nigg Pfeffer, the

outfielder who, when he connected, sent the ball so far
and high over the light standards in left that it could barely
be seen as it kept rising toward infinity. The question was
whether the ball might strike the tall smoke stack in the
back of Saint Joseph School, on the far side (the width)
of the football field behind left and center field. When
Nigg connected late in a game, the crowd would stand,
clap, scream, howl, and go home happy, we kids skipping
through the cemetery back to our cars. Chick Alles was
Nigg's only competition as a slugger. It was thrilling to
see a relative "knock the feathers out of the ball," as Dad
would say, circle the bases, and tip his cap to us at home
plate. I also remember Bob Thacker at shortstop and Junie
Schnarr in the outfield, but that may have been later, on a
different team. Willie Haas, whose mother was best friends
with my mom, was a smooth-fielding second baseman and
crowd favorite who later had a good run with the team, and
Jerry Schneider was a tall southpaw who could put a mean
"bend" on the ball.

Like many fans, we parked along Twelfth Street and
walked through the cemetery, between the tall tombstones
of the old German pioneers and clouds of mosquitoes,
on our way to the bleachers along the third-base line. No
doubt we sat in that section of the bleachers, near the top
row, because my father had severely injured a knee in a
car crash in the 1930s, walked with a pronounced limp,
and could scarcely negotiate the steep steps. I remember
the feel of his hand grasping mine, to steady himself, as

we were about to take our seats. We always arrived early,
to savor the festive atmosphere and see some batting and
infield practice. The chatter of the players, usually with a
German accent, never let up from pregame drills to the last
out in the bottom of the ninth, if the Reds had to use their
last turn to tie or win. Sitting high in the bleachers along
the third-base line put me in excellent position to jump up
and chase, in competition with classmates, after the many
screaming foul balls that came down the left-field line and
bounded toward the corner.

Directly behind home plate was the covered
grandstand where you could move if it threatened to rain
and you read the signs early and correctly and beat most
of the crowd in the race for shelter. The biggest section
of bleachers was behind and beyond first base, down the
right-field line, not far from which, set back, stood the
concession stand. There you could buy sodas, the sticky
dark-brown caramel Sugar Daddies that could suction a
baby tooth right out of your mouth, hot buttered popcorn,
and the cotton candy that "schmeared" your face before
some of it managed to melt in your mouth. There were
also hot dogs and chili dogs, smothered with mustard,
that would tie your stomach in knots and make you fart
all the way home and all night long and make you beg for
another Coke. Also available was Joe Palooka Bubble Gum,
sometimes so hard to chew that you were sure it was left
over from the previous baseball season.

Dad had been a pitcher on the Saint Henry Indians

team that played its games in a pasture and was especially
appreciative of the skills of the home team and opposing
pitchers. He was very partial to breaking balls, especially
the overhand curve ball then called "a drop." "Man, did
you see that ball drop?" he would ask, his voice rising in
admiration. "Chust like this!" And he would trace with
his right hand the down-curving path of the ball. After we
moved from East Fifteenth Street to Holy Family Parish,
to our property on Schroeder Avenue, we spent at least
half an hour every evening in the grass alley in back of the
garden playing pitch and catch. He worked very patiently
to teach me how to throw a curve, how to grip the ball with
the red seam between my index and middle fingers so I
could give it the proper spin as I released it, with a snap of
the wrist, and create a trajectory that might fool the batter.

"Here, watch me," he would say. Just barely five feet
tall and burly, he would wind up slowly, come from way
above, "on top of the ball," as the sportscasters say, and
throw me a ball that dropped a good six inches, right into
my glove. "You can do it."

And if a pitcher on the Reds, or on the teams from
Rockport, Tell City, or Owensboro delivered a curve ball
that left a hitter staring as the ump called "Steee-rike Thu-
ree!" or lunging in embarrassment, he noted, "See, that's
what a good curve ball can do. Fools the pants off the
hitter! Hooie!"

One episode from all those Sunday night games stands
out in my mind and has become a legend. Brute Hoffman,

big, burly, and loud, but friendly as anybody could be, had a ferocious temper. He was also as stubborn a Dutchman as could be found in Dubois County. As I have mentioned, when he could no longer catch, he turned that responsibility over to his cousin Eddie and became the manager.

This one particular Sunday night, Brute was not at all satisfied with the ump's calls, and his protests grew louder as the game progressed. The Reds were losing and had little chance to get back into the game. Our hitters looked pathetic, all of them. As Brute grew angrier and louder, the ump grew sorer and sorer until he finally turned toward the bench and gave Brute the mighty heave-ho, "You're outta here!"

"Good, you blind son of a bitch, I don't wanna be in the same ballpark as you!" We fans loved it and hooted and hollered in Brute's defense. Everybody knew the game was a goner, and we wanted to have some fun.

"Got news for you, Mr. Loudmouth, you won't be in the same ballpark as me for long if you keep it up." Boos, catcalls, hisses, from the bleachers, on both sides of the field, and the grandstand beyond.

Finally, Brute lifted his heavy frame off the bench and took a seat in the bleachers at the end of the right-field section, where we could hear him bark, way above the din of the crowd, every time a pitch was called.

When he could take it no longer, the ump called time, flipped his mask off, walked over to the screen separating him from Brute not far from the concession stand, and

My father in his Saint Henry Indians uniform, circa 1920.

with a rousing sweep of his right arm, threw our manager
all the way out of the ballpark. They stood eye to eye,
the high screen between them, jawing back and forth as
we applauded, until Brute finally grabbed his jacket and
walked through the open gate beyond the concession stand,
yelling every obscenity he knew, his back turned toward the
ump. He lumbered beneath the huge oak in the right-field
corner, beyond the fence, and stood at rest behind the gate
in right field, in view of everyone in the park, players, fans,
and home-plate umpire.

When the ump called the first pitch a ball, Brute's
shriek of, "Why you miserable sonovabitch!" rose above
all the noise in the stands, as if the hot curse were a huge
spitball mortar lobbed at the umpire. The man in black
threw his mask down so hard it bounced off home plate,
and he signaled, defiantly, in Brute's direction, that the
game was over. We were all standing, laughing so hard we
had to support one another. That night, the night the game
was called, Brute became a local legend.

26

The Bus to Saint Louis

The first time we made the trip, we left before the light completely broke. I don't know how many times I was lucky enough to go to Saint Louis to watch the Cardinals play in the old Busch Stadium, probably not very many altogether, but the first time stands out. It was mostly fathers and sons, and we were going to see a major league baseball game, the ultimate thrill. The trip may have been tied to the Jasper Little League system, for I do remember that my Cubs manager, Vic "Peewee" Bohnert, was along, and I think that Carl Seng, manager of the rival Dodgers, was also part of the group that made the pilgrimage. Most of us were regulars at watching our semipro team, the Jasper Reds, play Sunday night games, and some of the players, including my relatives, were on that bus, probably in seats of privilege near the front.

Of course, everybody knew everything about baseball, which was a religion to us. We all knew who the high priests were, who was going to get into the Hall of Fame, the Pantheon of Greats, the Afterlife. We kids all bought and traded baseball cards, to us a variety of holy card, which meant that we memorized batting averages, RBI's, home run totals, number of wins and losses, etc., and recited statistics as if saying a litany: "Blessed is holy Stan Musial, saint of the corkscrew stance and the wicked line drive, thirty-two home runs, forty-eight doubles, 121 RBI's, may God shine His light upon him." My father liked to point out that Stan the Man went to mass and communion every day. Some of Dad's buddies, including "Mophie" Schuetter, a short man who walked with a bad limp, were on the bus. Whoever was along, was in hog heaven, or hardball heaven, to fine tune the metaphor. What could be better?

We also had our liturgical chant: "Ninety-nine bottles of beer on the wall, ninety-nine bottles of beer, if one of them should fall, how many bottles of beer on the wall?" There may have been ninety-nine bottles of beer in coolers, and all of the bottles of beer in the coolers were iced down, right there in the middle of the aisle of the bus, within reach of any adult on either side of that aisle. Every time we went around one of the countless curves on the old highway to Saint Louis, most of which were eliminated when they put in Interstate 64, we heard the beer bottles and the ice shift and clink together. Those coolers were made of metal, not the Styrofoam or plastic current today. By the time we returned to Jasper after the double-header, lots of the ice thawed out, the sound of those bottles of beer clanging in the coolers changed pitch, and the singing turned into snores. The music of the beer bottles dropped a register, as most of the bottles were full of air. The service was over.

On one of the trips, and it may have been that epic first one, which seemed destined to last a full week, not just one Sunday in summer, we went to watch the Cardinals play the Dodgers in a double-header. We were going to pay tribute to Dodger first baseman, Gil Hodges, son of Princeton and Petersburg, both towns not far away in southern Indiana. Nothing better than saluting a local hero. He was one of us, represented us, did us proud, even if our bus included more Cardinal than Dodger fans. Some of us thought Hodges might acknowledge us, maybe even talk to us. He never did. Maybe the organizers of the trip did not make the necessary contact in advance, but word did get to us in the stands that they were trying to reach him in the clubhouse. They did not succeed. The fact that a group of Hodges fans from Jasper, Indiana, was in attendance was announced at the ballpark or on the radio or both, but I do not believe that any contact was made. We were crushed, but we pretended that everything was okay.

I do remember that when we got to our section of seats along the right-field line, one of our two seats had a view partially blocked by a big steel girder. My father, who was disappointed, but kept his feelings to himself, except for his body language, took the obstructed view. "Can you see?"

he wanted to know. I nodded yes, felt guilty, but not guilty enough to let him have the better view.

Another baseball ritual we shared was attending *The Babe Ruth Story*, starring William Bendix, at the Astor Theater, the only time we ever went to a movie together. I held my breath so that the movie about Dad's hero, the rough-hewn, unpolished, but lovable Babe, the Sultan of Swat, would last forever. Dad was forever a Yankee fan, mostly because of his love for the Babe, and could not bear to miss any of the World Series games on television. We watched the games at Aunt Frieda and Uncle Otto Hoffman's home on Rieder's Hill, Newton Street. In the days before we owned a television, that, too, was a religious ritual.

Two of my best memories of Busch Stadium have to do with Stan the Man. In one scene, I am sitting along the third-base line, so that I have a good view of where a home run would travel on its way to the roof of the right-field pavilion. Anything not hit onto the roof was still in play, as a wire mesh covered the front of the stands. Musial had not had a very good day, as I recall, and all the fans were standing, yelling encouragement. Musial coiled into the corkscrew stance, the pitcher wound up, fired the ball, and The Man unleashed a swing that connected and sent the ball rising, rising until it landed on the roof. Bedlam. Another scene takes place later, when I am in Busch Stadium with fellow senior scouts from Troop 185, Holy Family Parish. Along was my best friend, Mick Stenftenagel, who was an All-American football player in high school and a basketball star who went on a scholarship to play under Whack Hyder at Georgia Tech University. Also along were Jim Gutgsell, Kent Kunz, and Buddy Friedman. We came on Saturday, spent the night in a hotel, and got to the park early to watch batting practice. We had seats in the left-field bleachers, right at the wall.

The great Musial was catching fly balls in the outfield, just below us. We were leaning over the wall, begging him to throw us a souvenir. "Come on Stan!" I begged. "Flip me one!"

"Okay," here it comes," he replied. He motioned as if he were going to lob it up, I leaned down to grab it, and he pulled back.

"Hah hah, fooled ya!" he chortled.

After that epic first trip to Saint Louis in the bus with the fathers and sons and the musical beer bottles, I slept well through the night, got up early the next morning with visions of grandeur crowding my imagination, and after Dad drove off to work, I headed down to the rock road in front of our house for some big-league baseball. I picked up my favorite stake, which was cut to a V at the bottom, scraped out a plate on the crown of the road with the point at the bottom, wrapped my hands around that V, in a lefty stance, in a tight corkscrew. Left field was the front lawn, with an orchard of apple and pear trees beyond. Right was a blue-green expanse of rye growing in a field that belonged to Holy Family Parish. Center field was the rock road itself, leading down to Charlie and Laverne Schuck's house.

With my right hand, I flipped a rock in the air, grabbed the stake with both hands, and skimmed one that whistled over the top of the rye in right. It felt so good to pull! Then I repeated the cycle, but this time I delayed my swing a bit, trying to hit it straight away, as the best hitters so often do. After I connected, the rock headed straight for that telephone line crossing the road and I knocked some imaginary dirt off my cleats with the stake, turned around, and batted right handed in imitation of my new hero, Cardinal third baseman Ken Boyer, he of the slick glove and mighty bat. It was the bottom of the ninth, the score was tied, and I had not had a very good game. I flipped up a rock with my left hand, quickly wrapped both hands around the bottom of the stake, took an uppercut swing, and lofted one toward the pear and apple orchard way out there in the recesses of left field. This one was gone, I knew it, took off for first, jogged around the bases, and, as I landed on home plate, I lifted my cap to the crowd. They were all standing in left, right, and center. I bowed, and they cheered even louder.

Now the fathers and sons could climb back on their bus and take off for the hills of southern Indiana. Let the beer bottles sway and clink as that bus veers around the curves. Lights flip on in small towns in southern Illinois and southern Indiana as the bus heads on its way back home.

27

The Holy Family Owls

You could not grow up in Jasper, Indiana, and not love basketball. The most famous date in the history of the town, 1949, is the year the Wildcats won the state championship. That was also the year Saint Joseph School caught fire, an experience I remember quite vividly, as we watched the glow of the terrifying flames from our upstairs window on the west side of our house on Fifteenth Street. Whereas that fire receded in our collective memory and went out, the championship experience blazed and soared to the level of legend. Coach Cabby O'Neill became a demigod and every little boy learned how to knock the eye out of the hoop his dad attached to the garage or suspended from a pole in the driveway.

It's no wonder that decades and a thousand miles away from that championship season of 1949, I became addicted to the film *Hoosiers*, which starred Gene Hackman as the gritty, tough-talking disciplinarian coach who took his small-town team all the way and won the state championship on a last-second shot. Though I never became much of a basketball player, Hoosier Hysteria is in my blood. After I saw the movie five times, the old legend of 1949 coursing through my veins again at each showing, I finally bought a videocassette copy so that my children and I could watch this Indiana story whenever we want, as often as we want, in the basement of our 1920s house on the North Shore of Long Island. Later, I bought a DVD version of the film.

Every time I see *Hoosiers*, the goosebumps rise on my arms and I feel that old tingle in my fingertips. I remember the flick of the wrist, the spin of the ball as it left my fingertips, and the swish of the ball through the net. I am back on the playground of Holy Family School shooting hoops by myself for as long as I want at one of the goals. I bounce the ball, bend my knees, shoot, get the rebound if I miss, let the ball roll back to me if it goes through the hoop and the net, and shoot again, maybe spin around the next time, move, gradually, in a semicircle from one side of the court to the next. Not many experiences feel better than having just the right touch and hitting everything you throw up at the circle of iron. There is something heavenly about the feel of the ball as it leaves your fingertips with just the right spin and arch and the swish it makes, over and over, as it hits nothing but net. You exist in a realm outside of time. Who cares what time it might be? How long you have been there? What anyone else might be doing? What may have happened at home earlier in the morning or at school the day before? This is eternity! Swish, bounce, bounce, bounce, swish, bounce, bounce, bounce, swish!

"Norb, time to come home to eat!" my mother cries out from the back porch, breaking the spell but giving me time to sink one more long one before I dribble back to reality. Ah, swish!

SCHOOL DAYS 1956-57
HOLY FAMILY

ABOVE: *The Holy Family Owls, 1956, left to right: Mick Stenftenagel, Larry Stenftenagel, Bill Gelhausen, the author; back row: Ron Schneider, Ken Greener, Dave Blessinger, and coach Kenny Blessinger.* LEFT: *Eighth-grade school picture, pink and black shirt, flattop emerging.*

When I was in the sixth grade we formed a team and played a game against a team from Saint Joseph School. This was the school I attended for four years while we lived on East Fifteenth Street, and now we were the country upstarts from the new parish and school out in the boondocks—the hicks, the hayseeds, the "shitkickers." What a vindication, what sweet satisfaction it was, to beat the city slickers, my former classmates from town, 31-28. I emerged as the high-point man with a whopping total of eleven points. "I think we must have talked about that game every day for at least two weeks," I said in a twenty-two-page autobiography I was required to write the fall of my senior year at Jasper High School in the legendary Jack Leas's English class. Leas served as the inspiration for my becoming an English teacher and writer.

In the seventh and eighth grade, the Holy Family Owls, as we came to be known, played in the Diocesan League. We played our games in the old gym at Saint Meinrad Archabbey and drove the half hour to each of the Sunday afternoon games packed in the pastor's blue Plymouth station wagon. Our audience consisted of ourselves and our coaches. It was a monastic experience that I loved. I was a guard and averaged twelve points a game, mostly on the strength of a two-handed set shot that, even then, was way out of fashion. Oh, the bliss of that swish, which feels twice as good when the ball spins off the fingertips of not just one hand, but both hands in harmony! As both baseball and basketball player, I felt an obligation to conserve the traditions. I loved to keep my eye on a curveball until I could see it hit the bat, loved to hit the ball the opposite way to right field; and I loved to arch a long two-handed set shot so gently and gracefully that it swished through.

I did not have, nor cared to develop, the other talents and skills required to make up the complete player, and after my freshman year in high school I dropped basketball and concentrated on baseball and football. I did not feel natural on the basketball court, was self-conscious about the acne that spread not only over my face, but also my shoulders and arms, and was relieved not to have to work on skills that I realized were only mediocre. After I quit, I was told the coaches wanted me to stay because of my "leadership ability and positive influence," but I did not care to lead or serve as model from the bench, where I belonged.

I never, however, lost the urge to watch a good game of basketball and was thrilled to cheer my classmates on to victory in the yellow-brick gymnasium on Sixth Street in Jasper, where Larry Bird later played some games for our rivals from Orange County, and have not forgotten how to shoot Hoosier hoops. Even though I wrecked my right shoulder playing high school football and my left shoulder is not far behind the right in pain from bursitis and tendenitis, I can still put the right spin on a basketball if I give myself the time and practice to restore the touch. Swish, yes, swish!

28

The Woods behind the House

When we moved into our new house across the
rock road from Holy Family School, the woods behind
our property was still wild. A logging company had cut
down some of the most valuable trees before we began
construction of the house. We nevertheless believed we
had intact woods as our playground.

To say the woods was behind the property is not
completely accurate, for it was also part of our 100 foot
by 200 foot lot. When we bought the property, there were
stumps left where tall trees had stood in the area that
became our huge vegetable garden, about one-fourth of
the lot. Because Dad's left knee had been badly damaged
in a car crash, he could not pull out stumps. Mom, the
tough farm girl, took over, would not give in, and would not
accept defeat. She wrapped a rope around the whole stump
or a stubborn root and pulled like a mule until we heard
a pop and crack, something gave, and the stump's spirit

and hold were finally broken. When Mom had vanquished
enough stumps, we piled them together, poured coal oil
or gasoline on them, struck a match, and watched the pile
poof into angry flame. Sometimes we threw a cattle skull,
evidence that the area had once been a farm, onto the fire,
and Dad explained that all the ashes would be good for the
garden. Because it had been part of the woods, the earth
we turned over was dark and rich, a wonderful loam, a
humus that wriggled and breathed.

Sometimes Mom and Dad left Ed and me in the
black 1949 Chevy parked alongside Schroeder Avenue, a
rock road, with the nose of the car at the crest of the hill
pointing toward Justin Street down at the bottom. If I knew
they were working far enough away not to hear, I pushed
the starter button on the dashboard, the car chug-chugged
back and forth, and Ed and I giggled. Holding the steering
wheel with one hand and pushing the starter button with
the other, I pretended we were pulling away.

Mom and Dad loved woods so much that they made
sure we had trees close to the back of the house that our
new neighbor, Marcus Kuper, known as a builder of good
solid houses, was putting up. Right outside my upstairs
bedroom window was a huge, stately sugar maple, not
far from a beautiful white oak. In the forks of these two
living poles of our childhood, our parents wedged a pipe
from which they suspended a wooden swing that creaked
back and forth over the fieldstones they laid out as a
patio. Summer nights, with the windows wide open, we

heard turtledoves coo and, as we were about to fall asleep, the haunting cries of a hoot howl sent our way from a beech tree next to the creek in the valley in the middle of the woods. In the morning we woke up to the canticles sparrows, robins, and cardinals sang in the sugar maple. Sometimes during the day we heard the "Bob white!" calls of quail from within the cover at the edge of the woods between our lot and Charlie Schuck's property.

Because the woods behind our new house, between the houses on Schroeder and Hopf avenues on the north and south, and behind Justin Avenue on the west, were so full and deep—tall sugar maples, oaks, beeches, pig hickories, sweet gums, black cherries, sassafras, a few sycamores near the creek in the middle, and many pawpaw saplings—we had a boundless but protected leafy and shady kingdom in which to play. "The woods are lovely, dark, and deep," Robert Frost wrote in a line that reverberates every time I read it, and "there was pasture enough for my imagination," wrote Henry David Thoreau, in a statement whose implications continue to expand as I think of the miniature cosmos and eternity we lucky children had at our disposal.

Ed and I, and later Lenny and Mary Lou, could meet our cousins Tony and Janie at the creek, the midpoint between our houses, the crossroads and center of our kingdom of play. Jim Weyer and his brothers might join us from their path that joined our north-south axis, and Johnny Schuck and his brothers, though they were younger, could also come from their house near ours and meet us

Top: Krapf brothers playing in the leaves with Trixie, 1954. Above: Picnic-table stagecoach, 1954: The author riding shotgun, cousin Tony Krapf driving, Ed holding Trixie, and Schuck children concealed in the back compartment. Right: Cousin Tony Krapf and Ed come out of the woods shooting.

under our vaulted ceiling of leaves. Even if it started to rain, we were protected until the dripping started, but even that was an anointing we enjoyed when we felt it splatter on the tops of our heads and the back of our warm necks. In the spring, there was a canopy of mayapples at our feet in every direction, dogwoods bloomed not far over our heads and, when summer was full, the green roof stretched over our heads wherever we wandered.

If we wanted, we could break through the protection of the woods and arrive at somebody's house for ice water, lemonade, or Kool-Aid® and a raid on the garden. Sometimes we would come to our house, get a loaf of white bread from Mom, go into the garden, pull out some shallots, descended from our great-grandmother's garden, hose them off, and make ourselves an onion sandwich, washed down and cooled off by great gulps of ice water. In season, we could also walk into the tomato patch, pull off the biggest, ripest tomatoes on the stalk, take a big bite, feel the hot juice splash against our palates, and swirl it around in our mouths before swallowing. Sometimes we even stooped to making ketchup sandwiches that left a dark red crust around the corners of our mouths as we ran back into the woods to play cowboys and Indians, hunt with our bows and arrows or cap guns, make a lean-to shack or teepee, or bury treasure we had stolen from somebody's house.

In the depths of those woods, we once smuggled a pack of Camels we bought from a cigarette machine at Sternberg's Construction Company down along the highway. Being the older brother, I stood as lookout and told little brother Ed when the coast was clear for him to approach the machine, drop the quarter, pull the slot, and run out of the building with me. The sound of Sternberg mechanics giggling followed us all the way to our hideaway deep in the woods where we lit up, puffed, coughed, and smashed the rest of our cigarettes out with the tips of our cowboy boots.

We played until we heard Mother ringing a cowbell to announce that the meal was ready, or crying out from the back of our lot, in a singsong voice, "Soup's on, come and get it. Soup's on!" She sometimes waited there while we huffed up the path and joined her at the top of the hill in the alley, where she was humming "The Tennessee Waltz" or "You Are My Sunshine."

"Did you have fun?" she wanted to know.

29

Morning Rounds

My father and I spent many hours hunting squirrels together, starting when I was about nine, but because of his debilitating knee injury, he could not do the extensive walking required for winter hunting. Even though we kept two bird dogs in a pen in the woods behind the house, I can count on the fingers of one hand the number of times we hunted rabbits and quail together. When I was in sixth or seventh grade, I began to do something that many boys in the parish did—trap rabbits.

At first I scavenged several old wooden boxes, the kind that grocery stores threw away in those days. With the help of my father, I cut a trapdoor opening in the top, and with his tools carved three sticks to form the figure-four trigger holding up the box, which I weighted with a heavy flat stone. The box or trap rested on a simple wooden platform. As I became handier with the tools and savvy about trapping, I built my own traps with scrap lumber from a nearby mill.

The night before the season opened in mid-November, my father bought some inexpensive apples that I cut in half and used as bait on the long end of the trigger. Every morning, well before I had to leave for the Catholic grade school across the rock road from our new house, I awoke to the sound of my alarm, dressed in old clothes and rubber hunting boots, and walked out in the brisk morning air to check my traps. Over my shoulder I slung a burlap bag, into which, carefully using work gloves, I put any rabbit that had nibbled at the bait and caused the heavily weighted box to trip and fall. There was never more than one rabbit per morning—most mornings there was nothing but standing traps. The biggest disappointment, however, was to see from afar that a trap was down, feel my hope building up uncontrollably, only to discover that a rabbit had gnawed a hole through the bottom of the box where it joins the platform and squeezed out to freedom. Some mornings, as my heart thumped, I opened the trap door to a box, only to find an opossum squinting up at me from the darkness within. In those cases, I kicked the box over so that the creature could escape without harming me.

When I did find a rabbit crouching in a far corner of the box, I sometimes feared that I was not equal to the task of lifting the squirming and scratching creature through the narrow opening on the top of the box and snuggling it, safely, still kicking, into the burlap bag. I knew that a good hunter or trapper was not supposed to think about whether an animal he hunted had feelings, but I could not help but feel sympathetic. If I did trap a rabbit, it was my grim responsibility to kill it, clean it, and dress it so that Mother could fry and bake it for the family with dark gravy, onions, mashed potatoes, and vegetables from the family garden. Despite the mixed feelings I had about taking the life of an animal, I was proud to be able to help feed the family.

When I started high school, I no longer kept my rabbit traps because I had to drive into town with my father on his way to work, and we had to leave too early to allow me time to check traps before school. Holy Family grade school was just across the street from our house, a proximity that had allowed me the freedom to leave for school at the last minute.

Perhaps because I no longer kept traps, winter hunting became more important. At the time, the parish pastor, Father Othmar Schroeder, was a friend of the family, and my parents had given him permission to build a dog pen in the woods behind the house so that I could feed and care for his two spotted bird dogs. From early Saturday morning until supper time, I hunted with those dogs back by the Patoka River, even when it became fiercely cold and the picked soy bean fields, into which the swollen river had overflown in the lowest areas, became crusted with ice.

One Saturday I hunted longer and harder than usual, with no luck whatsoever, and because I hated the thought of returning the dogs home without having seen a single quail or rabbit, I decided to make my way over the ice to a patch of groundcover that looked promising. I walked gingerly over the ice toward the cover that I was sure concealed at least one rabbit or a covey of quail, saw the ice begin to crack, and splashed into the cold water that seeped into my boots and left me shivering all the way home.

I was careful not to show my discomfort that evening to the family as we sat together talking in the television room, and went to bed early, feeling slightly feverish, in the hope that a good night's sleep might restore my strength. Christmas vacation was about to begin, and I couldn't bear the thought of missing one day of hunting because of a bad cold. Sometime during the night I became aware of a pain in my chest and my breathing began to sound heavy, then raspy. In fear I tried to call out to Mother, who was sleeping downstairs, but no sound but a terrifying rasp came out of my mouth. I could not tell if I was dreaming, or actually suffering, and therefore became even more frightened.

Then I had a dream that I remembered when I woke up. I was running, too slowly, along a railroad track in pursuit of a caboose on the back of which people stood, encouraging me to catch up with them and come aboard. After struggling, I came nearer the caboose, but at the cost of aggravating the pain in my chest, which by now was severe. The people on the caboose were extending their outstretched hands toward me. I summoned up my last reserve of energy, lunged, and then discovered that the train had passed around a bend and was no longer in sight. Then I could hear myself wheeze, the caboose reappeared, and the scene repeated itself with the same result. Each time I came nearer the caboose, the faces of the people trying to help me became large and vivid and I could read their expressions of frustration. They wanted to help, but could not.

In the morning I somehow stumbled down the stairs and staggered into my parents' bedroom. They quickly called the family doctor, who rushed out to the house to examine me and announced that I had acute pneumonia. That was the least eventful Christmas vacation I ever had. It took a long time to recover. I could not hunt with the bird dogs any more that season and have never forgotten the pained expressions on the faces of those kind people so determined to pull me aboard the caboose.

30

Queenie and Ike

When Mom and Dad bought the property on Schroeder Avenue, the lot next to it was owned by a man from Louisville named Meschede. He had built under the trees a makeshift shack we called Meschede's Cabin. Meschede used this cabin, which had no indoor plumbing, mostly for weekend trips to the outskirts of Jasper. Eventually, someone reported to the authorities that Meschede was in violation of the ordinance banning outdoor toilets in the new Hasenour Addition. He received a notice from the courthouse, became discouraged, and decided to sell the lot to Dad and our neighbor down the hill, Charlie Schuck, and took down the cabin.

Meschede never became our neighbor, but two bird dogs, Queenie and Ike, took up residence not far from where the cabin once stood. Father Othmar Schroeder, our pastor at Holy Family Parish, liked to hunt, especially quail. He was friendly to Mom and Dad, often came to our house for dinner, and after I started to do work for the parish and Holy Family School, counting the collection, cleaning toilets, and mopping and waxing floors, he took me hunting for squirrels and rabbits on his relatives' farms. When he bought two bird dogs, he asked Mom and Dad if they would be willing to keep them for him, they said yes, and we built a pen and large doghouse in the woods in the vicinity of where Meschede's ill-fated cabin once stood.

Father Schroeder did most of his quail hunting during the week, which meant that I had the dogs to myself on Saturdays. The young, frisky Queenie, a Llewellin setter, and Ike, a veteran English setter whose patience was endless, were an interesting pair. To Ike fell the responsibility of training me as a hunter of birds, while I trained Queenie how to point and hold. In the late fall I awoke early, ate a breakfast of bacon, several fried eggs, and buttered toast Mother prepared, put on my weather-proof hunting suit and red leather hat, two pairs of wool socks, and boots, rested my shotgun, an automatic .20 gauge I borrowed from my Uncle Arthur Krapf, on my shoulder, and headed out the back door. Queenie started to yap when she saw me, Ike boomed out his basso profundo, and they pawed at the gate of the pen as my strides, as long as I could make them, ate up the distance between us.

One crisp, cold November morning, when my puffs of breath hung in the air, Queenie jumped a rabbit in the brambles right behind the pen just seconds after I opened the gate. I boomed a shot that sent the rabbit rolling until it flopped to a stop. As soon as I picked it up and turned around, I saw Mom running toward me. She had been standing at the kitchen sink washing breakfast dishes when she heard the shot and was convinced her eldest son had tripped and shot himself.

Our triangle of boy and young and mature dogs hunted through the little woods behind our house, then a wild and tumbling patch of fallen trees, pokeweeds, and blackberry brambles beyond the woods, and finally cut across Brames Road and sauntered along the creek that ran through a big field. Almost every time I walked along that creek I flushed a Wilson's snipe.

One bright fall day when the sky was intensely blue and the air was pure, we crossed Brames Road in full view of some house builders, who were hanging from the rafters watching, with skepticism, the too-young boy hunting with the two beautiful bird dogs. Ike came to a point and held rock steady, while Queenie pointed, then fidgeted and edged forward, wagging her tail slowly. Such a moment, so full of anticipation, comes to seem frozen in time, especially to a young boy when he is inside it. "Whoa, Queenie," I said as calmly as possible, "Whoa!" Suddenly a covey of quail thundered into flight. After a split second, one of the carpenters hanging from his perch in the rafters, as if he were positioned in the first row of the balcony of a movie theater, where the old-pro reviewers sit, boomed out a harsh adult command, in an accusing tone: "Well, shoot, *boy*!" I was leading a quail, pulled the trigger just about then, and a quail plummeted to the ground. A few feathers spiraled down in the cold air after it. Ike sauntered over to the beautiful little bird, which was no longer living, and ever so gently took it into his mouth and brought it to me. He looked up at me as if to say, "Way to go, kid! You're going to get it! I'm proud of you!" I never turned around to look at those carpenters, but I could feel their gaze trained like crosshairs on the back of my hunting coat.

"Good dog," I said to Ike, rubbing the fur between his ears. "See, Queenie?" I asked as I let her sniff the dead quail before I put it in the pocket of the lined hunting coat. More often than a good hunter was supposed to after he shot a quail—or rabbit or squirrel—I slipped my hand into that pocket in the back of the coat and touched the soft, warm creature. Sometimes, I took the quail out and examined the delicacy of its feathers, beak, and claws in the glow of sunlight.

My favorite place to hunt with Queenie and Ike was an area of woods and fields, often planted in corn or soybeans, owned by a bald and toothless farmer, Leander Giesler. One day after school I walked to Giesler's aged, ramshackle farmhouse, which was torn down a year or two later, knocked on the door, and asked if he would please give me permission to hunt squirrels in his little woods. When I told him who my father was, he stared at me a while, as if weighing the pros and cons, and said in a faint voice, "Yeah, I guess that be okay." During August and on Saturdays in September and October, I rode on my bicycle early in the

Dad spreads birdseed on the patio. Behind, in the woods, is the pen and dog house where we kept the bird dogs Queenie and Ike.

morning, my Uncle Ed Krapf's .16 gauge, double-barrel
balanced across the bars, toward a gate at the top of the hill
opposite Giesler's farm house. I parked my bike alongside
the gate, crawled over the boards, and walked across
the open field into the woods, where both fox and gray
squirrels lived. This was the first squirrel-hunting woods I
ever discovered on my own and had to myself. Part of these
woods backed on the Patoka River, and part of it rose to a
hill and a fencerow that included my favorite persimmon
tree, which I visited every fall for the soft orange fruit my
mother made into such a tasty pudding.

Sometimes at the edge of that field near the woods
stood a row or two of corn stalks with ears of corn still on
them. At times the edge contained soybeans that had not
been harvested and I chewed the white soybeans. This area
had good cover for rabbits and quail. More often than I
should have, I shot rabbits instead of quail when I was with
Queenie and Ike. This was, of course, not a good example
for Queenie, who was happy to sniff and run after anything
wild. Ike would turn and give me a patient look, as if to say,
"Okay, boy, I'll give you that one, even though you're not
supposed to shoot rabbits around us. But I understand. I
was once a boy." Who was teaching whom? There was a
yellowish light of illumination and understanding in Ike's
soft and loving eyes that would stay with me. After giving
me that look and measuring the distance between himself
and Queenie, Ike would roll his eyes, turn around, slowly
break into a trot, and go looking for the next covey.

When we were hunting in that corner of Giesler's farm it was as though Queenie, Ike, and I had a universe to ourselves and unending time to explore it. I loved to take a break, sit down, and have them snuggle up to me on either side. I brought along a sandwich and an apple for myself, dog biscuits for them, and there was plenty of cold creek or river water for them to lap up. We usually made our way back to the little woods behind our house and their pen about the time the light was beginning to wane. There was a bond between me and Queenie and Ike, a level of understanding, a feeling of affection, and a mutual gratitude that was palpable. We were a community.

Probably the best reward I ever gave them and myself was in the spring, when the hunting season was not open but all three of us were bursting to get out into the woods and fields. I set them loose and they barked and I whistled and sang as we hightailed it all the way back to the Patoka River. Leaves were unfurling on the maples, dogwoods were in bloom, mayapples were coming out under and around the trees, wildflowers were sprouting up, and the leaves on the ground gave off the smell of duff. Everything was rife with the scent of sensual life about to explode and we three felt it. As we came to the banks of the river and stood watching the spring currents roil, we knew that the woods, the fields, and the river were ours. We could not have wanted any more of heaven.

31

Popcorn, Hickory Nuts, and Walnuts

There was always a special quality to the fall air and sunlight that led to a unique sharpness or intensity of perception and exhilaration. One of the things I did then was to take off with a burlap bag and walk to the popcorn field across the Jasper-Ferdinand Road from Knust's Grocery Store. I don't know who owned that field or who farmed it, but every year popcorn grew in it.

I waited until the field had been machine picked, walked along the highway in my high-top shoes, and veered into the field as soon as no cars passed and nobody was looking. I walked along the edges of the field, where the machine had not cut down all the stalks or picked them clean, picked the hard yellow golden ears, and dropped them into the burlap bag. At such a moment, the whole world was bright gold.

I felt some guilt for taking what obviously belonged to someone else, but at the same time I knew that to take what someone had overlooked or missed was to make good use of a bounty that would be left unclaimed, except for the animals that roamed the field at night. I was saving what would have been wasted and was proud to bring home a special treat for the family to eat on winter days. There is nothing like the sound of popcorn popping in the pan on the stove in the kitchen on a winter day as the smell permeates the house and you and your brothers and sister reach into the bowl to grab handfuls and stuff your face with mounds of puffed-up buttered whiteness until your belly swells with happiness. Such ecstasy allows not even a trace of guilt for harvesting and sharing the goodness someone left unpicked in a field.

One Sunday afternoon every fall, after the first frost, when the weather was clear and the air was crisp, the whole family piled into Dad's 1949 Chevrolet with several burlap bags in the trunk, drove past the field where I had harvested my treasure of popcorn, and turned right at Knust's Store onto a rock road that wound and climbed into the hills. Rocks kicked up against the bottom of the car as we sat in the backseat, squirming, eager to explode into the woods. At the top of a hill, Dad pulled off the road on the right at the Blessinger farm and coasted to a stop under a black walnut tree. We flushed away from the car like a covey of quail, each with a burlap bag over our shoulder, glided down the hill, and landed under the first shagbark hickory, where the pearl-like hickory nuts had burst from their hard green shells after striking the ground. We stuffed our burlap bags with the frost-white nuts, found other shaggy trees whose bases were sprinkled with nuts, turned around at the bottom of the woods, and ran back up to the top of the hill, the harvest banging against our backs inside the burlap bags. By then it was almost dark, and Mother would stop at the edge of the woods to clip some of the orange-eyed bittersweet that she kept in a brown jug in the living room.

The Krapf brothers hulling walnuts.

On Sunday afternoons in the winter, we cracked open those white shells, picked out the meaty kernels, and chewed the rich, wild-tasting nuts, or put them in a bowl for Mom to use in baking cakes and cookies or fruit or vegetable breads. Dad always had a glass of his reddish-blue homemade wine with his nuts, sighing after every sip. Then he might put *Rhapsody in Blue* or the *Nutcracker Suite*, his favorites, on the stereo, sit in the white-oak rocker that had been his father's, and stare out the picture window while he tapped his foot. We could hear Mom humming in the kitchen as she stirred something cooking on the stove.

My favorite autumn activity was to gather walnuts on my own, leaving home with a burlap bag and hiking toward the walnut trees I had already staked out and observed for several months. I had a favorite black walnut tree, not even five minutes from the house, old, gnarled, and almost always laden with fruit. When I picked up the walnuts, most of them were an intense green, for they still were in the husks that gave off such a pungent odor. Some of the walnuts had begun to turn brown, and I had to be careful not to touch the deepest brown, unless I didn't mind having my fingertips darkly stained. I loved the smell of those husks, so strong, wild, and smacking of the depth of the forest, even though this tree was not far from a house and near a concrete block building that housed Spindler's Sheet Metal Company.

I dumped my heavy bag of walnuts near the picnic
table in the back yard under the trees, gave the hulls time
to harden and darken, and then placed them on a brick
and hammered off the husk. I was always careful to wear
work gloves. If I didn't, and maybe even if I did, I could
end up with some dark stains that were almost impossible
to remove. The walnut stain that we buy today in our
hardware stores in suburban malls to brush onto veneers
is made from the rotted hull of the walnut. Some of my
classmates at Holy Family School looked down upon
anyone who came to school with stained fingers, which
marked them as hicks. It was as though our fingers had
indulged in forbidden sex and the walnut stain was a sign of
our transgression. Yet, in some way, to have a dark walnut
stain on our fingers was to wear a badge of distinction: we
were tied to the woods, to the fields, to the country, to the
earth, to wild animals, to all that is dark and unknown. We
couldn't have said that, but many of us understood it. Part
of me was proud to be seen with this stain, this badge, on
my fingertips.

Besides, the oily meat of the black walnut, hidden
within the dark, hard, furrowed shell, was deliciously
wild. I liked it better than the English walnuts available
in the stores—pale, thin shelled, mild, and bland. In the
taste it lays on the tongue, the black walnut packs the
concentration of the wild and the forbidden.

32

The Martin Box

My father took great pride in building a deluxe martin box for the new house built on a hill at the edge of the woods. Every year the raising of the martin box and the return of the martins were major events for him. He never said so, but I suspect his father, Benno Krapf, who operated a steam-engine sawmill and threshing machine, was also a devotee of the purple martin. Dad built his own "martin box," as he called it, at the workbench in the basement furnace room. It was, in effect, a royal apartment complex for purple martins, with all the amenities a prince or princess of the species desired. There were two stories, each apartment having its own perch and walkway, and there were four equal sides of four cubicles on each of the two levels. Dad painted the wood white and the trim dark green. The roof, replete with asbestos shingles, was sloped, just like a real house roof. When the construction and painting were finished, he mounted the box on a metal pole that he painted silver, and repainted every season in preparation for the Great Return.

In the first years of our stay in the new house on Schroeder Avenue, near the driveway he cemented a three-sided metal stand or base, through which he drilled holes and painted silver. Every spring it was an important ritual to raise the martin box. We put the base of the pole against the cement and the back of the stand, raised it gradually and bolted it in place. Then we stepped back to admire the site and the handsome accommodations.

Dad was always very proud, and a little anxious. "Gonna have martins," he proclaimed. But we could tell that he was trying to make it happen by sounding extra confident. We could hear the uncertainty underlying the proclamation.

During those first few years of our life in the new house, the martin box was well populated and my father was in bird heaven. After he cleaned the box and touched up the paint, we raised it again, and he started his watch of the local skies. He set up a green lawn chair at a location that gave him the best perspective for the first approach of the season. At the sign of the first dark wing, he exclaimed, "Here they come!" Most of the time, he was right, but when he was wrong, the silence was heavy until the first tenants arrived. Then he began his count. "Got twenty-two so far this year!" he boasted. If they were slow to arrive, he complained, "I chust don't understand! What more can a guy do?" He shook his head, turned, and limped away from

the pole, but the smile returned when the martins came
back.

Cutting the grass when the martins had young ones
was always a challenge, for the mothers did not like the
noisy invasion of their territory. I remember pushing the
power mower as fast as I could up and down the hill near
Schroeder Avenue in a rush to finish the lawn before
baseball practice began late in the afternoon. My eyes
were on the ground, my mind was on baseball, and I was
stunned when a dark-winged bird buzzed right over the
top of my baseball cap, squawking mightily, not once,
but several times. Goosebumps raised up and down both
tanned arms. I had a healthy respect for the dive-bomber's
motherly instincts and loyalties, but I felt wronged. After
all, I was being a good son.

Eventually, Dad and Charlie Schuck decided to buy
and split the vacant lot between the two properties, and
not long after that development Dad moved the martin
box to the beginning of that half lot. Maybe that's when
things changed for the worse. I don't recall if the relocation
coincided with the resumption of his "nerves problem," as
Mom called it, but the loss of the colony of martins, such
an important part of his psychic life, left a mark on his
demeanor.

"I can't figure it out," he told us. "Linus Dick down
the road has ten pairs this year. Syl Giesler has five pairs in
that new box he put up for the first time this year. Maybe
that's what the problem is. Maybe ours went to him. Surely

My father's martin box, left, 1954. Later he moved the location of this box to the front lawn near the driveway and added another box in the back of the garden.

there's nothing wrong with my box!" There was no doubt that Dad took the absence of his beloved martins as a personal loss and a personal rejection. The house stood there, high atop the pole, empty for several seasons, and then he stopped putting it back up. We stopped watching the sky, did not see the swoop with bit of straw in beak, no longer heard the squeak of the young, and stopped waiting for the birds each evening as they returned to the roost.

On some level, Dad accepted the defeat and eventually turned his attention to the softball games played across the street on the field that Holy Family Parish laid out. Seated in the dark-green metal chair that had been his perch for watching and listening to his martins, Dad puffed on his pipe and watched the sons of his friends club the softball into the recesses of the outfield. Every once in a while, a high arching foul ball landed about where the martin box once stood, right next to the driveway. Dad would limp over, pick it up and roll it down the hill and back across the road.

33

The Lampert Farm

We followed the Dubois Road to Jasper Lake, but instead of climbing to the top of the hill where Camp Carnes, the Boy Scout camp, was located, we turned left onto a rock road. After a couple of bends in the road, we turned right onto a lane that wound up the same hill that stretched to Camp Carnes and beyond. This was a dirt and sandstone lane that sometimes incorporated a huge flat rock as its base, sometimes red sandstone ground down to a near powder by truck, tractor, and car tires, and sometimes yellow dust. The car groaned and whined in the pale light of early morning as we climbed that winding lane in low gear. Eventually we reached the crest of the hill, the lane took a sharp turn to the left, and we pulled into a barnyard that looked like something out of a painting by Albrecht Dürer. A rooster was crowing, hens were clucking, hogs were lying in their wallow, and a few calves were bawling for milk. Not far from an old tractor that had metal spiked

wheels, we parked the car, got out our hunting vests and
guns, and walked up sandstone steps to the front door of
the old farmhouse, probably built when the first Lamperts
arrived from Germany.

A heavyset old German woman who was happy to see
us came to the door. She and Dad exchanged greetings in
German, Mrs. Lampert smiled at me, and she wished us
luck hunting squirrels in the woods that sloped down from
the farmhouse on the other side of the big hill. My father,
who loved to speak German with farmers, may have gotten
permission to hunt their woods when he sold the Lamperts
life insurance. I was nine or ten the first time he took me
there to hunt squirrels. My gun was a .22 single-shot, bolt-
action Winchester rifle. The sight I used to line up my
target was open (no telescope for the beginner) and my
ammo was high-power hollow points. I may not have been
the world's greatest marksman, but I was keen to learn
how to hunt and shoot squirrels. I had heard my father talk
about his sojourns in the woods near the village of Saint
Henry in Lindauer's Woods that came to take on legendary
status the more stories he told about hunting in its groves.
He and his father and brothers all entered that woods to
hunt and came home somehow expanded, in ways I was
just beginning to comprehend. I wanted to experience the
same kind of growth in skills and development of character
and spirit I sensed resulted from going out into the woods.
I wanted to learn, wanted to become somebody.

We descended down a path into the corner of the woods and stood still together. I watched my father as much as I watched the trees as a model of how to hunt: where to train my eyes, how to cock my ears, what to look and listen for. One of the virtues of hunting squirrels is that you do not talk. You must communicate in ways that do not require speech. About the only time we broke that holy rule was after one of us shot a squirrel, when we would sit on a fallen log for a break. Dad broke out his pipe, stuffed it with Prince Edward tobacco he poured out of a flat red tin, put a match to the bowl, and sent out puffs of smoke that drove the mosquitoes away. He would look up at the trees, point out a nest here, a hole that was a den there, a cluster of hickory nuts on a shagbark nearby, and whisper as he nodded with emphasis: "It's got squirrels here." He was translating from the German, "*Es gibt hier.*" My father was never happier, more at peace with himself, than when he was in the woods observing the shape of trees and looking for tell-tale signs of squirrels. Squirrel hunting was good therapy for the pressures of selling insurance and the depression that sometimes haunted him.

He used his finger like a teacher's pointer to pinpoint cuttings lying around the base of oaks and shagbark hickories. He raised his first finger for me to listen when he heard the sound of cuttings begin to patter through leaves as they fell to the forest floor. At first I watched him to see where he was looking, to find the flick of a tail or a sign of movement on a far limb where a fox squirrel might sit grinding his teeth on a hickory nut or acorn. It was apparent that when he located a squirrel, he tried to get me into position to have a shot before he fired. Sometimes he pointed out an imaginary path I might follow to put myself in the right spot, without snapping a twig or scuffling in dried leaves and scaring the squirrel away. I had to avoid making any noise with my feet, I had to keep my eyes and ears wide open for signs of movement or location, I had to get myself to a spot where I might have a view of the exact location where that squirrel was eating, at the same time that I had to avoid finding myself in a position that allowed the squirrel to see me.

That first time we were in Lampert's woods, Dad and I heard cuttings fall from a tree like fine rain. I was not sure what kind of tree it was, but later he told me it was a black gum. Dad seemed to be getting closer and closer to the point where he might get a shot, but I could not see anything and felt discouraged. He was going to shoot a squirrel I was not even able to see. As I was watching him sneak closer and closer, I heard and saw some branches bending not far away from me, but in the other direction from where Dad stood peering up into another treetop. There in full view of me was a fox squirrel moving through a tree at a leisurely pace. He had not seen me! I cocked my rifle, raised it, tried to put the body of that squirrel right in the middle of that open sight, and thought I was squeezing the trigger. It seemed an eternity before the gun fired with a loud crack. I may have jerked as I supposedly squeezed. I may have led too little or too much as that squirrel kept moving. When I fired, it leaped into another tree and disappeared. Dad gave me a look of surprise mingled with disappointment. His squirrel also disappeared when I fired at mine.

A few years later, Dad bought a Fox double-barrel twelve gauge with full and modified barrels. There was an engraving of a pheasant rising in flight before two hunters on the metal part of the stock. Dad kept that gun and all others cleaned, oiled, and polished. This Fox was his pride and joy. The first time he ever used it, we returned to the Lampert's farm one Thursday afternoon. We hunted slowly, methodically down the slope of the woods, beneath tall oaks and large hickories, and came to a little hollow between rolling hills near the back end of the woods. We were standing there, eyeing the trees, training our ears, when something came loping over a small hill. Dad raised his new Fox shotgun and pulled the trigger, dropping a red fox in its tracks.

Late that morning of my first hunt, when Dad and I returned to the old farmhouse to load our guns and vests in the trunk of the car, Mrs. Lampert lumbered toward Dad with a grin on her face. While we drank from tin cups the cold spring water she drew from a well, she explained to Dad in German that when I fired my first rifle shot at that first squirrel I had found on my own, she was standing at the sink washing dishes. The crack of my shot was so loud that it startled her, almost causing her to drop a dish. "But I missed!" was all I could think. I had not yet learned that what you bring back home from squirrel hunting in the pouch of your hunting vest is not nearly as important as what you find and leave in the woods.

34

Aunt Tillie's Farm

Once a year, my father and I would drive to Saint Henry, where he was born and grew up, to go squirrel hunting in the woods on the farm of his Aunt Tillie Luebbehusen. Usually, we would go there on Labor Day. This was always a happy return for my father and it was uplifting for me to be along. Great-aunt Tillie, a large and slow-moving woman, was born in Indiana but spoke no English. It was easy to see that she and Dad had a special relationship. From the moment that we pulled up in her barnyard, after winding along the gravel lane that brought us there from the rock road heading south into Spencer County that began near the edge of their farm, the time we spent on Aunt Tillie's property was time in another world. Aunt Tillie and Dad communicated with an ease that relaxed us all. There must have been a series of such welcomes and exchanges going all the way back to the time when Dad was the boy who hunted in the fabled Lindauer's woods located behind his father's house in the village of Saint Henry, founded shortly after the Civil War. (Aunt Tillie's father, Joseph Luebbehusen, married Mathilda Lindauer.)

Aunt Tillie came lumbering out to the car and welcomed us, she and Dad talked in German, and I listened and understand most of what they said. When Aunt Tillie asked how I was doing, the first thing I did was nod. If I said a few words in German, she smiled, but if I answered in English, she understood, smiled, also nodded, and said, "*Ja, gut!*" Her smile had a sweetness to it that was as pure and bright as the light in her blue eyes. There was a heaviness in her flesh and a largeness in her bones, but her spirit illuminated the area where we stood in the red-sand barnyard. One of those times we came to hunt squirrels, my father must have praised the rare white lilies in bloom along the edge of her vegetable garden. When we returned from the woods, Aunt Tillie presented us with a bunch of those lilies, bulbs and all, which she had dug and wrapped in moist burlap. I am sure my father did not ask her to send some of those prize lilies along with us for Mom.

Aunt Tillie had a son named Josie and a daughter named Marie living with her in the old farmhouse, the center of which had once been a log cabin. Josie, who always dressed in overalls except when he went to church, was tall, scrawny, and oddly sunburned in the face, even in the dead of winter. A painfully shy man, he disappeared into the barn or headed into the field shortly after shaking

The second Saint Henry Church, built in 1910, as seen in 2005.
Benno Krapf cut the timber for the church with his sawmill.

our hand and offering a few words that came out of his
mouth as if they inflicted pain on the man who spoke
them. After Josie died, they found jugs of wine and bottles
of moonshine stashed in the barn, sheds, and at the base
of corner fence posts in the fields that he plowed. Marie,
a cheerful, energetic slip of a woman who kept her hair
tied back tight in a bun, hovered in the kitchen like a
hummingbird whose wings never stopped whirring. When
she spoke, it was as though I heard a delicate song that
came from a distant place. Music was a major part of her
life. She played the organ at the Sunday high mass in the
Saint Henry Church. How appropriate that she died of a
heart attack one Sunday while her delicate but deft fingers
were pressing the keys of the organ! She was forty-one.

As Marie stopped breathing, she was surrounded by
the dozen handmade black-oak music stands my father
and grandfather created as a gift for the church choir in
the winter of 1925, when Benno Krapf's steam-engine
sawmill and threshing machine were shut down for the
winter. Decades later, when my father told me the story
of how he and Grandpa had made those stands, I asked
if he would help me get one to preserve and pass on as a
family heirloom. We drove from Jasper to Saint Henry and
used Bernitha and Bing Werne, who cooked the priest's
meals, cut the parish grass, and rang the church bells,
as intermediaries. The pastor, who was not from Dubois
County, informed me I could buy one of the music stands
for twenty-five dollars, which I had to borrow from Dad.

CLOCKWISE FROM ABOVE:
Double stained-glass
window in Saint
Henry Church donated
by my grandparents
(right) and Benno's
brother and Mary's
sister, who married one
another; the black-oak
music stands built for
the choir loft by my
grandfather and father,
then age sixteen, in the
winter of 1920; the site
of the first Saint Henry
Church, the building of
which began in 1862.
Beyond the cedars and
the cemetery stands
the "Sears & Roebuck"
house built by my
grandfather, Benno
Krapf.

Bing and Bernitha, who lived in a modern brick house across the street from the church, knew that my father had been born in a room above the saloon, operated by my great-grandparents, that once stood on the same site. Bernitha, a kind and loving soul who appreciated my devotion to family history, blushed a shade of purple when she received news of the price from Bing.

Irony aside and the cost be damned, it makes me feel good to have standing in my living room a simple work of art my grandfather and father once made of local wood with their own hands for a church that my grandfather helped build with his sawmill, pro bono. My spiritual satisfaction deepens when I reflect that men and women have stood together reading sheets of music that rested on this handcrafted heirloom, singing in harmony as my musical cousin, Marie, gave heart and soul in contributing her talent at the keyboard to praise the beauty of God and the Creation they all loved so intensely.

Not far from where Marie slumped over the organ in the choir loft, there is a magnificent double stained-glass window with this dedication: "FAMILY/BENNO & MARY KRAPF"; the other, "ALPHONSE & ELISABETH KRAPF" (Uncle Alphonse was Grandpa Benno's brother and Aunt Lizzie was Grandma Mary Luebbehusen's sister); yet another, "FAMILY/NICHOLAS & BARBARA HOHL (Marie's grandmother, Barbara Barth, married August Luebbehusen, after the death of her first husband). In the cemetery near that beautiful church in the quiet village,

Benno and Mary Krapf, my grandparents, and Johann
Krapf, my great-grandfather, are buried, as well as Marie's
grandfather, August Luebbehusen, my great-grandfather.
Not far from the front door of that church huddle two rows
of ancient cedars, between which the first Saint Henry
Church once stood. As a little boy, my father stood there
and watched flying squirrels glide from cedar to cedar.

One Labor Day, Dad and I departed from our custom
of making the ritual return to Aunt Tillie's alone and invited
our pastor, Father Othmar Schroeder, who had been
taking me hunting in his brother-in-law's woods. Instead of
stopping at the farmhouse, we drove directly to the woods
in Father Schroeder's blue Chevy station wagon, parked
just inside the woods along a lane, and got out to put on our
vests and load our guns. I was first. As I finished loading
my .16 gauge double-barrel, I looked up at a small hickory
nearby to see what I might find. "Oh," Father Schroeder
said in a teasing tone, "you might as well not bother to look
up there. You won't find a squirrel this close, so soon!"
Right about then a fox squirrel came slowly down the trunk
to check us out. I tried to steady the bead at the end of my
gun on its head so that I would not splatter the body with
buckshot. "For heaven's sake, go ahead and shoot!" said
the priest, grumpily, with a lack of patience unbefitting a
mentor. I fired and the squirrel flipped to the ground.

The three of us went our separate ways after we walked
together into the heart of the woods. I later heard Father
Schroeder shoot, and after about an hour I met him at a

TOP, LEFT: Tombstone of my Uncle Jerome, who died in Germany near the end of World War II. TOP, RIGHT: Tombstone of my great-grandfather, Johann Krapf, born on December 10, 1830, in Kreuzthal, Lower Franconia, and died on October 12, 1893, in Saint Henry. BOTTOM: Tombstone of my grandparents.

place where two fences joined at a right angle. I was doing something that a seasoned hunter would or should not do in the woods. I took the fox squirrel I shot out of my hunting vest to admire its russet tail and creamy yellow belly. Father Schroeder announced that he had also shot a squirrel, which I asked if I could see. When he stuck his hand into the pouch behind his back, he discovered that his "dead" squirrel was still very much alive and could have given him a nasty bite with those devastating teeth and clawed his flesh. "Don't tell anybody," he pleaded. We both knew that if word got out that he carried a living squirrel around the woods in his hunting vest, he would be disgraced. I said I would not tell, and I have kept that promise for fifty years, but an author has got to tell the truth, sooner or later, no matter what the consequences. As Huck Finn once said about a dilemma he faced as a boy, on a famous and unforgiving river: You're damned if you tell and tortured if you don't! The afterlife looms heavily over your head and the smell of fire and smoke is never far away below.

When gentle Aunt Tillie died, they laid her out in a Sunday dress in a wood coffin in the parlor of the old farmhouse. I like to think that her son, Josie, built that coffin. I remember standing there in the parlor, gazing at her sweet German face that was in such repose. I thought of the German words that bound her and my father forever together. Aunt Tillie did not speak English, but she did speak the language of pure spirit grounded in solid earth.

Her every action spoke a love that was not in need of being proclaimed from the pulpit.

35

The Shape of Trees

Although he did not often come back home with many squirrels in the pouch of his hunting vest, my father loved to go hunting in the woods. Later I understood that what he loved most about hunting was the serenity and the calm palpable in the earliest hours of the morning when, with the slightest hint of light dawning behind the outline of trees, the natural world begins to awaken and sing. Or in the evening when a hush settles over the forest, darkness begins to descend, and the silence expands. Several hours of absorption in the rhythm of the southern Indiana woods, morning or evening, created a welcome reprieve from the pressures of selling insurance, or, before that, working in a wood factory. When he began to take me with him when I was nine or ten, I was not fully aware of what drove him to the woods, but I appreciated the nature and depth of its pull. I may not have understood the tensions tearing at him that led to several "nervous breakdowns," but I could see why he found the woods so soothing. That time together in the woods of Dubois County, precious to me then, has become invaluable to me now.

We shared a love of quiet and listened together to what the woods had to say. We walked slowly, as any good hunter must do, we paused, and we listened. I loved it most when, after we had hunted for a while, we sat down together on a log or a stump and Dad lit his pipe, sending regular puffs of smoke rising into the early morning sunlight slanting through the trees. Sometimes we broke the sacred spell of silence but only with hoarse whispers. Dad might point to a clump of dead leaves in the fork of a tall shagbark hickory or a dignified old oak, indicate that it was a squirrel nest, and whisper his favorite refrain: "Got squirrels in here." I would be reassured, even though we had not yet seen a single tail, and resume gazing at the trees with a renewed interest. I scrutinized every branch, fork, and clump of leaves for a glimpse of red—for the sight of the puffy red tail of a lazy fox squirrel, sated with nuts, napping in the area.

My father had acutely sensitive ears and could detect from an impressive range the sound of a squirrel cutting on a nut and dropping its shell, in tiny pieces, from the top of a tree down through the branches and leaves to the forest floor. From the time that I began hunting with him, however, I was blessed with better eyes and accepted it as my responsibility to see a squirrel before he could. Together, I told myself, we worked very well. Sometimes

when we were circling a tree on which we knew a squirrel
was eating, I became edgy for fear that I might step on
a branch or a twig or clump of dead leaves and frighten
the squirrel away, or I became impatient and feared that
my father would shoot before I, who had not yet killed a
squirrel, would ever have a chance to see one.

Once, in my quiet agitation, I did crack a twig beneath
my foot in such a situation, and Dad frowned and gestured
from the other side of the tree for me not to move any
more. I was ashamed of my performance, felt I had let him
down, and concluded that I would never become a good
hunter. Only later, after I became more experienced, did I
realize that he was working hard to arrange for me to be in
the right position to get the first shot

One day I finally did shoot my first squirrel, and my
father was deeply pleased. He was standing farther away
than I from the big hickory, one he had many times shot
squirrels from, off to the side where he knew the squirrel
would come off the big tree if spooked. Every year the base
of this huge hickory tree was blanketed with cuttings. Dad
later told me that his father would come to this same tree,
pick out the squirrel closest to him, shoot, reload, and wait
at the same spot until the cutting began again. This was
before there was ever a season on squirrels.

That morning I was moving close to the point where,
while the cuttings rained down, I thought I would have a
clear shot. The sun was beginning to brighten behind the
branches of the shagbark hickory as branches and leaves

took on individual shapes against the backdrop of sunlight. I followed the cuttings back up to their source in the sunlight, located the branch on which the squirrel must be sitting, but could not find the exact spot. Then I noticed some movement along the branch, raised my .410, sighted, dropped it to chest level, raised it, and sighted again. The fox squirrel had gone out for another nut. I was tempted to shoot while it was moving, but at the last minute I pulled away because I knew I must not take any chances. I wanted to eliminate all the odds and wait for a sure shot. I waited, as my father had told me to do, and as the squirrel sat facing me I could see the creamy yellow of its belly fur. The cuttings started to fall again, I raised the .410 and tried to steady it in the center of that creamy yellow.

My gun was swaying as it did in the dream that haunted me when I would come home from the woods empty handed. I would locate the tree after picking up the patter of cuttings from a good distance away, size up its position in relation to other trees onto which the squirrel might jump, circle around toward the side where the cuttings were dropping, and wait for it to move into the open. Sometimes I waited for half an hour, sometimes as long as an hour. Then finally the squirrel appeared, bigger than I expected it to be—more like a full-grown raccoon or baby bear than a fox squirrel. It moved into full view on an open branch, I cocked my gun, raised it to eye level, and tried to steady it on the creamy fur of the belly. When the bead was lined up for a split second with the yellow fur, I closed my eyes and pulled the trigger. Nothing happened. No explosion, no recoil whatsoever on my shoulder. The hammer had locked. While I struggled to unlock the mechanism, the squirrel saw me, disappeared behind the trunk of the tree, and leaped away from a branch on the backside of the hickory.

This time I took my eye off the sight for just a moment to steady my vision, then centered the bead back on the target and squeezed the trigger. "*Squeeze*, don't pull," I remembered. Even so I couldn't help but flinch; as my index finger began to squeeze, my eyes closed. Then inside the darkness of my head came the explosion and I felt the .410 push back against my shoulder. It seemed like my eyes were closed forever and I was falling down a bottomless silo.

Before I could open my eyes I heard a crashing in the big tree. I looked up and saw a furry blur plummeting through limbs and leaves of the hickory onto a sapling below. I'd never heard such a racket in the woods. The squirrel thumped to the ground, rustled, then stopped moving. From where I was standing, I couldn't see where it had landed. I was afraid it might drag itself away and die in a hollow log. I broke open the .410, ejected the empty shell, and tried to insert another in case I had to groundshoot the crippled squirrel. The smell of gunpowder lodged in my nostrils and my throat throbbed.

"There he is!" my father blurted. "Over there near the base of the tree. You got him. You got him good. He came straight down. Let's go get him."

I was still in a daze. I couldn't believe I actually hit the squirrel sitting way up there in the top of the tree, couldn't believe I heard it crashing down and thump the ground. I expected to hear tiny feet scampering across dry leaves. I squinted across the forest floor toward the base of the big hickory, but couldn't see anything except a smoky haze. I felt slightly off balance. Then I saw my father squatting near a tree and a small reddish creature lying still between his feet. I dropped the .410 to my waist and walked over.

"Pick him up," he half whispered, half spoke in that hushed voice hunters use when they realize they've made a kill. "He's yours. Now you've got to learn to get him into the pouch of your new vest. Go ahead, pick him up." We were suspended together in the depth of the woods.

I couldn't believe that the wild animal that was so huge in my dreams was reduced to this size. Lying there on its back with its eyes closed, bright blood spotted across its yellow belly, its four paws limp, the animal looked so cuddly that I felt I must have violated some sacred law. I hesitated to pick it up. It might come back to life and sink those long curved teeth into my wrist.

"Go ahead," my father coaxed. "Pick him up. He's pretty, isn't he?" I nodded. I took the fox squirrel in my hands, gently stroked the soft dark fur on its back, flexed the bright red bushy tail where it joined its behind, and touched its black whiskers with my trigger finger. I felt a kind of awe I'd never felt before, not even in church, and was glad I didn't have to put my feelings into words.

I couldn't have explained how pulling the trigger had brought about this mood.

"Now let's get him into your pouch," my father reminded me in that hushed voice. "Here, let's sit down on this log. Now do it like this: stick your left hand back into the pouch and push it out through the right opening. . . . That's right. Now with your right hand take his head, feed it into your left hand, and pull him back into the pouch."

I followed the instructions. "Yes, you've got the idea," he said. "Now be sure to get his tail all the way inside. Somebody else might be hunting in these woods and could be trigger-happy enough to shoot at any piece of red they see. That's why I didn't want you to hold him in your hands too long. Some people lose all their sense when they get out into the woods. It's a shame."

I still didn't feel much like talking—an obscene thing to do at a time like that. The warm squirrel felt good slumped against the small of my back. The woods were quiet again, and it was as though I were sitting at the bottom of a cool lake squinting up toward the warm sunlight filtering down. I loved being so far away from everything, out in the forest, and didn't want to move.

Dad put a match to a pipe full of Prince Edward tobacco and puffed away. I breathed in some of the smoke hovering around my shoulders and felt a little giddy. "Just to keep the mosquitoes away," he whispered. We both knew this kind of joking protected us from talking about the feelings swirling inside us and appreciated the reprieve.

Above: Uncle Edgar Krapf (left) working at Link Belt in Indianapolis, 1924. Right: A photograph of Uncle Edgar, who died of a heart attack in Indianapolis, 1957.

Every time I'd been along when my father shot a squirrel, we sat like this on a log and watched the pipe smoke drift up until the stillness settled back over the woods. On such occasions, my father liked to point out the shapes of his favorite trees, which he traced with graceful gestures of his right hand. Later, driving the winding rock roads back toward town, he talked about the differences between the various hardwoods and the kind of furniture he and his buddies at the chair factory could make out of them. He always concluded, "I like to get out into the woods just to sit down for a while and study the shapes of the trees."

36

Silas and Fronie

I got to know Silas Mehringer through his brother-in-law, our parish priest, Father Othmar Schroeder, who brought me to the Mehringer farm to hunt squirrels when I was in grade school. To reach the farm, we had to drive from Jasper to the village of Celestine and beyond, turn right on a rock road, and climb high up a hill before turning left into their driveway. From their farmhouse on the highest hill in view you looked down on woods on three sides. Silas and Fronie (Veronica), who had no children of their own, were always happy to see me. In time, they invited me and my father to hunt in their woods whenever we wanted to come, and we came as often as we could.

Silas, who was short, burly, and strong, always had a grin on his face and a special light in his eye. To me, he was always kind and gentle, and he became a fatherly mentor. Known as the wiliest squirrel hunter who ever stalked the woods, he made it a point of passing on to me some of the secrets that would make me more successful in the woods.

"When you hear cuttings falling from a tree," he once explained, as we sat around the table after a meal of Fronie's roast beef, mashed potatoes and gravy, and green beans, "find where they hit the ground with your eye, then try to trace their stream back up the leaves to their source. Look for the sunlight. Concentrate on where the cuttings seem to be coming from, wait, and you'll soon see your squirrel. Be patient, and you'll get your shot."

"You know those three shagbark hickories in the back corner of the woods near Keusch's property," he said as I got out of the car. "They've been eating on them hard this week. Why don't you come along the fence toward them and wait next to that old black oak. From there, you can see all three trees and should be able to get a good shot."

If we came to the farm late in the season, he might advise me, "They've started to work on that old walnut at the back of the pond on the other side of the house, beyond the beeches. You know which one I mean, don't you? Good, now if one's eating on it and you can't get up close enough, pretend you're just walking along, not interested, stop suddenly, and shoot quick. You might fool him that way. Good luck!"

If I came back from the woods empty-handed, he always read my disappointment and asked questions about what I found on the forest floor beneath the trees where he knew they had been eating. He already knew how many shots I had taken, if any, and where in the woods I fired them. If I missed a squirrel, he wanted to know what kind of a view I had when I pulled the trigger and where the squirrel went after I missed. Then he would make suggestions on how I might handle such a situation the next time. Maybe I should approach that particular food tree from a different angle, wait a little longer to shoot, and make sure I saw more than just a tail before pulling the trigger.

If I knocked a squirrel out of a particular tree but couldn't find it, he always knew what hole in which nearby tree it might have escaped to. He told me where I might position myself next time so that I wouldn't make the same mistake again. "You have to learn from every experience," he said as he drew on his pipe. "You never want to leave a squirrel wounded in the woods or not find one that you've killed. That's not right."

Once, after we had hunted rabbits all day with his in-laws, the Schroeders, Silas volunteered to take me raccoon hunting that night, after a nap. We headed down the hill with his coonhounds long after everybody else went home. I had never gone night hunting. Silas hardly needed a flashlight to find his way in the woods, for he knew every den tree, ditch, hill, path, protruding root, boulder, and briar patch in the dark. We didn't shoot a single raccoon that night, but we had fun following the hounds through Silas's nocturnal kingdom. For me, this was the life of southern Indiana royalty, hunting all day in the most remote hills and deep into the dark woods in the wondrous night.

The last time I saw Silas was in the family room of my brother's tavern in Celestine, more than twenty years after I had done any hunting. I had sent him a postcard from Long Island telling him my family and I were coming home to visit my mother, we planned to come to eat dinner at Lenny's Tavern about 6:00 p.m. that Friday, and it would be great to see him and Fronie if they could meet us. We had gathered around a table, ordered our food, including the best German fries in southern Indiana, which my mother sometimes helped the cooks make, and I was taking the first sip from my schooner of beer when the back door opened. I looked up and saw Fronie push the door wide open to let Silas scuffle in. He was bent over, putting his weight on a cane, and shuffling toward our table. Both he and Fronie smiled the broadest smiles you could imagine.

Of course they came to our table and joined us for the meal. It took Silas a long time to decide what to order, for, as he said, "I ain't used to eating in restaurants. Can't remember when I did it last!" As Silas and I chatted, Fronie beamed her radiant smile. They were glad to see my mother again, meet my wife from Louisiana, and they both looked at my children in the same loving way they had looked at me when I sat at their table as a boy blessed with the opportunity to roam in their woods.

"I see he still likes to eat," Fronie observed to my wife with a grin. "He never turned away anything I set before him." Silas smiled.

37

Holiday Hunt

Once a year, between Christmas and New Year, I went rabbit hunting with Father Othmar Schroeder, his brothers, and his brother-in-law. I went alone because my father's knee did not allow him to do the kind of walking required for a daylong rabbit hunt. This must have been an important ritual for the males in the Schroeder clan, for they put aside their farm chores to go on this annual hunt, which was at least in part social. We hunted outward, in a kind of loping circle, from one of their farmhouses, where we gathered shortly after breakfast, cut back to the farmhouse for the midday meal, hot food that restored our energies, rested and visited for a while, then headed out in another direction, to hunt in another circle until dark.

Usually three or four barking beagles, straining on their chains, were released in the morning, and returned, happy but spent, tongues wagging, by the end of the day. My hand loved rubbing the space on the top of their heads between their long, floppy ears and my eyes loved gazing into their deep brown eyes. They recognized a compadre, someone who was thrilled to be in the field with them, and moved closer when I wanted to pet them. As soon as they were released, they filled the air with their yaps. When they jumped a rabbit, the sound shifted, the pitch rising, the intensity increasing, and you knew what was happening.

Most often there would be four or five hunters: Father Schroeder, full of nervous energy; Jerome Schroeder, his tall, gangly, and wiry brother, who had incredible hunting instincts and strode through the tall weeds and brambles like a giant; Silas Mehringer, my stocky, savvy squirrel hunting mentor, who liked hunting rabbits for the camaraderie but no doubt preferred his time in the woods; and me, the young hunter in training. Beloved Silas had a childless and drawn brother who insisted that it was wrong for their priest brother-in-law to bring such young boys, "who did not know what they were doing and were a danger," along to hunt rabbits or squirrels. The pastor, however, had a mind of his own and the other Schroeder men liked having a young would-be hunter along who loved the old ways that this hunt represented and wanted to learn from them the right way to do it. These were the regulars, the core group, but sometimes another male member of the clan would come along. I remember best the daylong hunts starting at Silas's farm east of Celestine and from the old Schroeder farm not far from Beaver Lake.

If we were walking through an expanse of broomsedge or other tall grass, we spread out in a line so that we could always see one another and never get in one another's line of fire. As soon as the dogs jumped a rabbit, we found spread-out positions to stand and wait so that one of us would get a shot when the dogs brought the rabbit around. You could hear from the regular or intermittent yaps of the beagles where the rabbit had gone and how far away it was. You could guess, even pray, which direction it would take, and then the direction it was coming in. If the yaps grew louder, you had to get yourself ready to shoot—the rabbit was probably coming your way. The idea was to position yourself in a spot that gave you a good vantage of where the rabbit might come, but also afford you some kind of protection from being seen. That meant you might get a good shot while the unsuspecting cottontail loped along, thinking it was outwitting and outpacing the beagles. Standing there in the cold as your breath steamed out of your mouth in puffs, waiting for the dogs to bring the rabbit around, gave you time to reflect on the beauty of the landscape, the sweet memory of other hunts, how many other rabbits you might jump and run, and maybe other subjects. The best hunters, however, always kept their minds close to home. You had to be ready. Sometimes a rabbit would be farther ahead of the hounds than you realized. The best hunters thought like a rabbit.

Tall, angular Jerome, who always had a grin on his face, had an uncanny knack of finding rabbits and shooting

them. Once he shot a rabbit running away from him with
a difficult shot and went to bend down and pick it up in
the tall grass. Before he stood up straight again, a sight you
could not miss, his shotgun boomed. I thought he must
have had a terrible accident. Did he trip and shoot himself
in the foot, leg, or worse? Suddenly Jerome straightened
up, holding a dead rabbit in each hand, a grin on his long
and narrow face. As he approached the rabbit he shot on
the run, he spied another sitting in a nest right near where
the first one stopped rolling. Jerome pretended that he had
not seen it, to keep the second rabbit calm, bent over to
pick up the first, and shot the second before he stood back
up. The other Schroeder clan members whooped in delight
at their brother's prowess.

My buddy Silas instructed me, tactfully, throughout
the daylong hunt, explaining how Jerome did what he did
and advising me on what to look for and what to avoid. He
also guided me on how to position myself in case I jumped
a rabbit myself or if the dogs started to run a rabbit, what
kind of location or "stand" to select for myself so that I
could be in a good position for a shot when the rabbit
came around. Whereas Jerome was primarily an instinctive
hunter, Silas came by his hunting shrewdness and savvy
more through reflection. Both, of course, were experienced
in the field and in the woods, and both, in truth, combined
instinct and reflection in how they conducted themselves
on the hunt. Once we were walking slowly along a ridge
where there were rabbit holes. I noticed that Silas slowed

down and moved gingerly. He reminded me of the bird dogs, young Queenie but especially the older Ike, when they caught the scent of quail. Suddenly Silas raised his gun and fired. From a pretty good distance, he had detected a rabbit huddled in the briars. He shot it in the head when he got closer so that the body would be clean of buckshot.

Once the group was in position for a long time while the dogs trailed a rabbit. It must have been an old, savvy buck rabbit that had been followed by dogs more than once. Just when the yaps came closer and got louder, they began to sound fainter and fainter, indicating that the old one had taken another turn. It felt like we stood and waited for hours. The temptation was to call out to the other hunters and ask what had happened, ask what to expect, but to do that would blow my cover. If the rabbit were anywhere nearby, he would be able to avoid coming into my view. That day I had not fired a shot, and just as I came to the conclusion that I would not get one at all, I saw the broomsedge moving out ahead of me. The yap of the dogs had not grown louder, which suggested that if a rabbit were coming through the grass, he had fooled the beagles. For a split second I saw the rabbit in an opening, then it disappeared again into the grass. I led where I thought it might be and pulled the trigger of the big single-shot twelve gauge I was lugging around. The recoil walloped my shoulder. Nothing happened.

"Didja get him?" somebody yelled. "I don't think so," I replied. "I couldn't even see him when I shot and I don't

see any sign of a dead rabbit." I had let the whole group
down and was dejected. Just then Jerome appeared on the
scene, stooped over, picked up a dead rabbit, and lifted it
up for me with a grin on his face. "Good shot, boy! Way to
go!" he said. "Thanks," I said, my toes tingling.

Every time I went on one of those holiday hunts
with the Schroeder clan, I had the feeling that time was
suspended and we were all part of something that went way
beyond us, beyond our time, and maybe even beyond our
place, but what I loved most was that these hunts took me
into places where I had never been. I got to see the woods
and fields, the whole rolling web of creation, from a new
angle. We hunted through woods and fields, briar patch,
and swamp, passing abandoned farmhouses, where broken-
down plows and harrows once pulled by horses rusted
beside clusters of weeds, next to abandoned wells, old
barns and sheds, crossed streams and creeks, stepping over
sandstone, walked along the tops of cliffs and down into
valleys, and ambled down lanes no longer used by farmers.

As I hunted with the Schroeder clan on those days
that carried us so deep into the country, across land that
belonged to a number of farmers, all of whom gave us
silent permission to hunt, I begged and prayed for time to
stand still and the day to never end.

38

The Gray Motorola

I have a First Communion photo of me with my godfather, Uncle Alfred Schmitt, and my godmother, Aunt Flora Schwinghamer, and another with my two grandmothers, Mary Schmitt and Mary Krapf. In both, I am dressed in my navy blue gabardine suit and a white shirt with big open collar folded above the jacket collar. I look like I could flap my collar and fly away. For both photos, we stood against the back of McDougal's concrete garage in our backyard on Fifteenth Street. We were having a backyard party, with cake, ice cream, and soda, and most of the relatives and friends who came gave me an envelope with money inside.

With this money, I later bought my first radio, a gray Motorola. It had a latticed front and big round dials. I don't have any memories of using the radio until after we moved the following year to our house in Sunset Terrace in Holy Family Parish, by which time it was a constant companion.

I could turn the round knobs and dial in music from far beyond Jasper, as well as listen to Harry Caray and Jack Buck announcing Saint Louis Cardinals games. The radio followed me around the house, from my bedroom upstairs to the sun room or family room downstairs, and, sometimes late at night, in the living room, where I tuned in the Cardinal games at the ungodly hour of 11:00 p.m. after the Brooklyn Dodgers betrayed everyone by moving to the West Coast.

ABOVE: *With my brother Ed on First Communion Day.* RIGHT: *First Communion cake, 1952.*

The music was mostly country, until Elvis exploded on the scene with his unique amalgam of country, blues, gospel, and rhythm and blues—a shot of energy that sent shock waves through the adult community. In addition to Elvis, I remember especially Marty Robbins's "El Paso," Sonny James's "A White Sport Coat," Hank Williams's "Your Cheatin' Heart," Brenda Lee's "I'm Sorry," and the heavenly harmonies of The Everly Brothers, my favorites, pulsing through the gray latticed front of that little Motorola. When Elvis burst on the scene, it was "Hound Dog," "Heartbreak Hotel," and "Love Me Tender" that came to town and apparently threatened my mother.

One day I was kneeling before the Motorola, which I had placed on the couch in the sun room, with my ear up against the speaker when Mother walked around the corner and came into the room. In her most understanding, tolerant voice, she asked, "Is that Elvis Presley?"

"No, Mom," I said. "This is Marty Robbins!" A couple of decades later, Robbins became one of her favorite singers.

When we still lived in town, I drove with my father to Aunt Frieda and Uncle Otto Hoffman's house for the World Series games, broadcast on television during the middle of the day. (We did not have a television until 1953.) At that time the World Series meant the New York Yankees, usually against the New York Giants or the Dodgers. We were Yankee fans, but after I acquired my own radio, I struck out on my own and became a Cardinal

fan, and Caray was my high priest. It did not bother me
that he was partial to the great Stan Musial and Ken Boyer,
my hero at third base, and little Red Schoendienst, Hoyt
Wilhelm, Vinegar Bend Mizel, and Sad Sam Jones, the
master of bad luck and heartbreak on the mound.

When we moved into our new house, Schroeder
Avenue was a rock road and I took batting practice in the
middle of that road with a flat stake, pointed at the bottom,
for a bat and rocks for the ball. I imitated Musial the lefty,
then turned around, became Boyer from the right, and
over the radio I could hear Caray announce that I had
just hit my thirtieth homer of the year and driven in my
hundredth run of this great season. On top of that, I was
having a great year with the glove, diving to both left and
right and coming up throwing with my gun of an arm. The
crowds hardly ever stopped roaring.

When I arrived back in the house, the music would
start up again on the gray First Communion Motorola:
"Dream, dream, dream" crooned by Don and Phil Everly,
"All I have to do is dream." Singing along with Sonny
James, I wore a white sportcoat and a pink carnation on
my way to the prom. Or sweet little Brenda Lee, with the
biggest, ripest voice in the world, told me she was sorry,
so sorry. I understood. I knew how to dream; I knew how
to forgive. I had great homebound instruction, coming
from my Motorola and the many teachers and models it
broadcasted into my ears.

39

Baby Girls

I was six and my brother Ed four when mother gave birth to our first sister, Marilyn. I don't remember the weather, but the day that Marilyn was born, January 25, 1950, must have been a very cold day. The birth of a daughter for a mother who has already given birth to two sons would normally be a time of great joy and celebration. We did not, however, rejoice. Instead, we grieved, for the date of my first sister's birth was also the date of her death. Marilyn was stillborn.

Mom and Dad's bedroom was downstairs, but my most vivid memory connected with the birth and death of Marilyn has me sitting downstairs in the living room, listening to something that was happening upstairs, at a moment when the house was eerily, heavily quiet. Grandma Mary Schmitt, who raised a family of six children by herself, came to be with Mom during this difficult period. I remember that I was sitting on the couch facing the stairs leading up to the open bedroom where Ed and I normally slept. As I sat there, in the sadness that seeped throughout the house like a crippling gas some invisible agent had released, I could hear the sounds of my mother's uncontrollable sobbing come down those steps. Quickly behind those sobs came the harsh and stern sound of my grandmother scolding my grieving mother. "Listen here," Grandma said, or words to this effect, "you have to be strong. Life is difficult, but you have two children to take care of and a husband. What do you think it was like for me to raise six of you after Dad died? Do you have any idea what that was like for me? I know this has been hard for you, but God wants you to be strong." Did I hear each and every one of those words my grandmother said in a raised

Tombstone of Marilyn, who was stillborn.

voice? No, but I did not have to hear her words in order to understand her message. Her tone told all. Even if I could not have explained it to someone else, I understood.

After learning that my first sister died when she was born, after hearing the tough advice my grandmother gave to my mother, I never had trouble understanding that life and death are part of the same process—are, in fact, inseparable. It has always been astonishing for me to realize that some people do not believe death is a part of life, life a part of death. I believe that anyone who grows up on a farm understands, on a primal level, the yoking of life and death, and nobody would have understood this better than Grandma Schmitt. I was upset with my grandmother, however, for being so harsh with my mother, and I felt rotten and helpless.

Normally an upbeat individual, Mother carried this heavy sadness with her for several years. I can remember my brothers and I kneeling around the bed in the guest bedroom one Lent saying the rosary, an exercise we found boring. We shifted from knee to knee. One of us boys showed our impatience by changing the tone of his voice, the others giggled, somebody inevitably farted, the rest of us laughed, and Mom cried, quietly. We looked at Dad, who made some excuse for her sadness, but I knew the cause. Mom lost the daughter she so badly wanted. It must have hurt to pray to the God who let that happen. I don't think Mom was capable of being angry at God, but the hurt in her heart healed slowly.

What healed Mom more than anything else, brought
the smile back on her face, and put the bounce back in
her voice, was the birth of my second sister, Mary Lou,
who was born when I was ten. The quiet crying during the
saying of the rosary stopped, even if the boyish breaking
of wind may have continued. If the mood of your mother
swings up, then the mood of the family also ascends. I
loved having a little sister. Once Mom went to Sunday
mass by herself, Dad babysat, and the inevitable came
to pass, as it were: Mary Lou's diaper filled with that rich
aroma of baby evacuation. Dad could not handle it. I took
over, wiped her little hills and valleys clean, pampered
them with powder, wrapped her bottom in the clean white
diaper, which smelled of the sunshine in which it had dried
on the clothesline, and closed it with safety pins. I did
this on more than one occasion. Mom had an instinctive
understanding of the importance of blurring the "gender
roles," as they came to be called, or of refusing to promote
one role over the other. She gave each of us boys a cap gun,
but she also gave us a doll. We played with both gun and
doll and never had the sense that it should be otherwise

Although the birth and life of my second sister, Mary
"Blue," "Tootie," as my Dad often called her, brought
joy into all our lives and she has remained close to me
over the decades, I have never forgotten about Marilyn.
Whenever I'm in Jasper, I like to visit her tomb and
look down at the words Mom and Dad had carved on it:
"Gone to be an angel." Even after more than fifty years, it

TOP: *My father with his three sons and baby girl, Christmas, 1954. ABOVE, LEFT: Mary at Holy Family School during my senior year of high school. ABOVE, RIGHT: Mary growing up. RIGHT: Mary's First Communion.*

seems impossible that the day of her birth is also the day of her death. How could anyone's life be so impossibly circumscribed in time? What would it have been like to have a sister some six years younger than I? Where would she be living now? What man would she have married? How many children would she have had? What would it have been like to have both of my sisters with me in this world? Is Marilyn a part of me now? Will we be joined in the world of spirit, as I believe we shall? Has she seen the world through my eyes, all these years? Does she speak in my voice? These are questions I have asked myself, but it occurs to me now that there is another angle I should have considered. What would it have been like for Mary Lou to have a sister who was three years older? How would Mary Lou's life have been different? What would it have been like for Mom to have two daughters?

Life and death are part of one cycle, is what I come back to. All that lives is a part of this ongoing cycle. I am blessed to have one sister as beautiful as the one who stayed in this world, the world I share with you. How poorer my life would be if that little baby girl had not been born to fill her diapers and our house with the rich aroma of baby girl.

40

Hauling Hay

When I was in the last years of grade school and the first three years of high school, I helped relatives and local farmers haul hay. The work was hard, the pay was not great (a dollar an hour), but I liked having the experience. I learned how to drive tractors and pickup trucks well before I was sixteen, the age required for a driver's license, made some money, and enjoyed being out in the fields. I left home early in the morning, full of energy and anticipation, worked hard all day, and came back home exhausted with a sunburnt neck, but was ready to get up and go again the next morning.

Sometimes I worked with my cousins on the farm near Ireland, Indiana, where my mother grew up, sometimes on the Grassland Hills farm of her brother, Uncle Bill Schmitt, then just north of Jasper but now a part of a subdivision, and sometimes with such farmers in Holy Family Parish as Rudy Vonderschmidt, Ray Hochgesang, and Willy Werner.

Sometimes I worked with my cousins Jim and Junior Hoffman, who, like his father, died young of a liver disease, or Alan and Howard Schmitt, and sometimes with friends Dave "Blitz" Blessinger and Mick Stenftenagel. We assisted the men who owned and managed the farms.

Usually, we would pull a wagon, or two wagons in tandem, behind a tractor. One guy was stationed on the wagon stacking the bales as they were thrown up, and two or three guys were in the field, on either side of the wagon, heaving the rectangular bales up onto the wagon as it approached. We had to grab the bale with two hands by the two strands of baler twine, which could cut or create blisters if you didn't wear work gloves or have calloused hands, get a good grip, and "let 'er fly." One lucky guy, usually the youngest, got to be the driver—a job I loved because it gave me experience at the wheel, usually with a hand clutch, and was a lot easier than heaving bales up onto the wagon, especially when the stack of bales grew higher and higher and it took more and more "oomph," as we called it, to get them up to the stacker. When the load was high, it took two of us, two hands on each line of twine, counting "one, two, three," to heave a bale underhanded all the way to the top. Often we took turns and rotated the various jobs. When we brought a load in to the barn, one guy unloaded the bales from the wagon onto the elevator, and another was just inside the entrance in the hayloft to take each bale off the elevator and sling it toward the stackers, who placed the bales in the right section of the loft.

The work always went best when we developed an identity and a rhythm as a team. If we competed, tried to show off our muscles or pulled against one another, an accident could happen. It was dangerous if the stacker did not do his job well, for the whole load could sway, the balance could be tipped, and the wagon could turn over. This was a distinct possibility if we had to drive from the field on a public road or highway to reach the barn. Perhaps because it was potentially dangerous, riding high on the wagon atop the stacked bales as the tractor groaned in high gear on the highway toward the barn was always exhilarating. Sitting up on top felt very good, because even though the air was warm, the resistance cooled us off. The chaff had a way of slipping down the inside back of our T-shirts out in the field and stinging our skin, we were always sopped with sweat when we climbed up the load to head toward the barn, and it was a relief to cool off and fun to wave to people who passed in cars. I liked it when people from town, as opposed to the farmers, recognized me, for I didn't like being considered a city slicker, as my godfather Uncle Alfred's sons sometimes sarcastically called us.

"Oh, you city slickers want to help on the farm," one of them might say. But they never passed up the opportunity to have extra hands.

When we came in for dinner, the main meal at noon, we splashed water on our faces and arms, or sometimes turned the hose on ourselves, and then sat down to a huge spread prepared by Aunt Elizabeth Schmitt or Aunt Lucy

Schmitt or Mrs. Vonderschmidt or Mrs. Werner. There
was usually pot roast or pork steak with dark brown gravy,
mashed potatoes, peas, beans, tomatoes, salad, bread and
butter, and always lemonade, pitchers of lemonade and
ice-cold water. We ate like hogs, as we said of ourselves.
There were still many bales in the field, a lot of work to be
done before we could stop for the night, and we needed
the energy that such good home cooking provided. There
wasn't much time to sit in the shade in the maple tree in
the barnyard, leaning back against its trunk. If it rained, the
hay would get wet, might not dry out properly, and there
could be a barn fire caused by spontaneous combustion.
There was pressure to get the job done, to get it done in
time, but there was also a special feeling of camaraderie.
We were part of something larger than our individual
selves, part of a cycle of the earth and its natural processes,
and eating hearty food and feeling our strength renewed at
the table was part of the cycle. We never got up from such
a bountiful table without thanking the cook several times.

One episode from my hay-hauling experiences stands
out in my mind. Blitz and I were working for Willy Werner
for the day in the area along the Ferdinand Road known
as Maltersville, located not far from Hall's Creek. It was
toward the end of the afternoon, we were rushing to finish
the job, and Blitz and I found ourselves alone, for some
reason. It may be that Willy, a very short and eccentric
Dutchman known for his expertise with four-letter
words, went back to the farmhouse to check on or fetch

something. Blitz and I were determined to get the job finished and done with, and it seemed that we would never succeed if one of us had to pick up and throw bales and the other drive Willy's old pickup truck and then stop it and stack. We were working on the top part of the field, which was mostly level, and decided that, just as we sometimes did with a tractor, we could put the pickup in low gear and let it run on its own. We tried it, decided it worked, and were making much better progress, when I looked up after heaving a bale and saw that the truck was picking up speed as the field began its gradual slope toward Hall's Creek.

"There she goes!" yelled Blitz. I took off running, made it to the left sideboard, crawled in through the open window, lunged with my outstretched arm, and applied the brake with my hand.

"Whew, that was close!" said Blitz. "Maybe we should say a Hail Mary."

We never told Willy. We already knew enough four-letter words.

41

A Gray Morning in March

"Come down, come downstairs right away, will you?" Mother called.

The sound of cutlery clinking in the kitchen below jarred my drowsy mind. At first I thought I must be dreaming, but when I opened my eyes and saw the gray, drizzly dawn pasted against the bare maple trees outside my upstairs bedroom window, I knew the voice was real. I staggered out of bed, wrapped a bathrobe around my shivering body, and started down the stairway one step at a time, like a sleepwalker.

Mother was standing in the kitchen, wearing a raincoat and scarf and holding an umbrella in one hand and a daily missal in the other. Her lips were pressed together.

"I'm going to early mass," she said. "You go into the bedroom and stay with Dad until I get back. It won't be long. Early mass is quick and I'll walk fast."

I would have asked for an explanation, but the way

her lips were pressed together and her hands grasped the umbrella and missal suggested something I didn't want to confront in words. Something about the way she was holding herself told me she was being courageous.

"Go ahead," she encouraged me. "He'll be all right. Just talk to him. I'll be back soon." As I entered the bedroom, I heard the outside door slam behind me. My father was lying on his back, on the far side of the double bed, as though he were floating on choppy water. He had a frightened look on his face, which seemed to say, "Pull me in, please pull me in," but I was standing on the shore without a lifeline. I settled myself into the bed as though letting myself down into cold water. From close up I could see that his eyes, normally pale blue and serene, were smoky and troubled.

He eventually broke the heavy silence: "Do you think I'm a good man?" The tone of his voice, usually calm, was aggressive. I was so taken aback I couldn't answer for awhile.

"Yes, why, yes," I stammered, sincere but sensing that I didn't sound convincing. My father had never asked me such a question, but the answer seemed so obvious that I couldn't imagine the reason behind the question.

"How do you know?" came the sharp, staccato reply, in a bitter voice that I didn't recognize. Fear shot through my bloodstream and began to knot up my stomach. I was trapped, felt it was unfair for me to be in this position, couldn't understand why this was happening to me.

My family, front porch, 1958.

Perhaps if I said nothing, if I pretended that I hadn't heard, my father would fall asleep, wake up with clear eyes and a soft voice, and we could get up, have breakfast, and talk about sports or hunting before getting into the car to drive to school and work. Only fifteen minutes ago I was suspended in a deep sleep from which I must have plunged into a bottomless nightmare. As my father stared relentlessly into my eyes, waiting for an answer which he must have known I could not give, the only thing I could do was look away into the blue painting of the Virgin Mary hanging on the opposite wall.

"How do you know," my father continued, "that I am a good man? Maybe I've done things you don't even know about."

Realizing that he must be driven by some force he couldn't control and which I couldn't understand, I knew that I had to find something comforting to say. I had to help. Maybe I could appeal to his deep faith in religion. Instinct, not reason, prompted me to try.

"Even if you did do something bad," I said with conviction, "you confessed it and your sin is forgiven and everything's okay." The words felt good coming out of my mouth. As far as I knew from what I'd been taught and experienced, I spoke the unalterable truth. Now he should be able to relax, maybe even fall asleep.

When I glanced over at his face, however, I saw that in the interval since I spoke, he was summoning up the strength to give vent to a reply that he'd thought out before.

"How do you know I haven't made bad confessions?" he asked. "If you do something bad and you don't admit it when you go to confession, then none of your sins are forgiven. You go straight to hell."

Years later I would learn that my father suffered from scrupulosity, a term I thought was positive. If you are scrupulous, you are determined and devoted to doing everything right; but as the term was used to apply to situations like his, it meant that he was too scrupulous. He thought he could never be forgiven for his sins, even if he confessed them to a priest.

The thoroughness of my father's argument and the finality of his conclusion left me speechless. Now I was trying to swim in a deep lake with a heavy stone tied around my neck. I remained silent, hoping we'd exhausted the subject and Mother would return home soon and know what to do.

Almost as though he were reading my mind, he asked me what Mother said before she left. Choosing my words carefully, I replied, "She told me you weren't feeling well and I should talk to you until she gets back from mass." He peered into my face, searching for evidence of a lie. When I looked at him to see how he took this explanation, I saw a face frozen in fear.

"Did she . . ." he began in a trembling voice. Then he blurted out a question as though all the words were one word he could hardly bring himself to pronounce: "Did she hide the butcher knife?" He paused for a moment,

SCHOOL DAYS 1957-58
JASPER HIGH

My freshman year of high school.

swallowed, and continued, "I told her she better hide the butcher knife or I don't know what I'll do. She promised she would. Did she?"

Now, more clearly than when I was waking up in my upstairs bedroom, I could hear the sound of cutlery rattling in the kitchen below. It was a relief to be able to say, without hesitation, "Yes, she did. She told me so."

For the first time that gray morning in March, I could see my father relax. He seemed to be floating on his own now, drifting but not in danger of sinking. We didn't speak, but turned our faces away from one another and waited, suspended in time, for Mother's return. I could hear the kitchen clock ticking away the early morning minutes, slowly. It was an eternity since Mother slammed the back door as she left to walk to church just across the rock road.

"Eternity," I thought. "What a long time to burn in hell."

As my eyes strayed around the room, I saw the pale blue painting of the Virgin again, a smaller red picture of the Sacred Heart standing on the chest of drawers, and a pair of candles on the nightstand flanking a vase containing palms that Mother burned during dangerous storms.

I could smell the palm burning once again. Around the bed I could see myself, my younger brothers, my sister, and my mother and father kneeling as we said the Lenten rosary in the evening, after supper. "Hail Mary full of grace the Lord is with thee . . . . Our Father Who art in Heaven . . . . Glory be to the Father and to the Son." The prayers were lodged in my mind as forms that were begun, completed, repeated by rote, and then forgotten except as forms.

Finally, I heard the back door open, feet wipe themselves on the entrance mat, and walk across the linoleum kitchen floor toward the bedroom.

"You can get up now," my mother said. "I'm back. Is everything okay?"

"Yes," I replied.

When Mother and I were in the kitchen, I said in a voice that made me sound older than the sixteen that I was, "I think he's resting now. What happens next?"

"In a little while they'll drive him to the hospital," she said. "Our Lady of Peace in Louisville. They'll take good care of him there. This happened once before, when you were little. You probably don't remember. He'll be just like himself when he comes back. Shock treatment can make a person like new."

I wasn't so little then as she made it sound. Dad was taken to Our Lady of the Peace for shock treatment not long after we moved into the house on Schroeder Avenue. I didn't know what the term meant when he left then for treatment, but I did recall that when he came back home he was extremely quiet and shaken. He did not act like himself. Once when he was driving the car into the garage shortly after he returned from the hospital, he saw my basketball in the space where he wanted to park the car. Instead of getting out of the car to put the ball in a safe place, he decided to nudge it out of the way with the front tire. As a result, I had a lopsided basketball I could not use.

On that gray morning in March, I did not like the sound of the words "shock treatment," which made me think of the way I felt when my father asked me how I knew he was a good man, but the quiet conviction with which my mother spoke made me feel that everything was in control and would work out all right.

"Thank God you just turned old enough to drive the car," she said. "You'll drive to school every day and drive me to the grocery. You'll have to be the man of the family now and help take care of your brothers and your little sister until Dad comes back."

The way she said this suggested that I would have to learn to swim in deep, dangerous waters, but that I could do it, and would do it well. I could not have seen it or said it so clearly then, but later it became apparent that this gray morning in March marked the end of my childhood. When my father was taken away for shock treatment not long after we moved to Schroeder Avenue, his worries and depression were no doubt intensified by the pressures he felt in having to pay off the increased debt for a new house. At that point, however, I did not understand the significance of his "nerves problem," as my adult relatives called it. This time around, though, my awareness was increased, and with greater awareness comes the passage into adulthood.

All the childhood experiences I have described in these pages were still with me that gray morning in March, were shaping me into the young man I would become. I felt equal to whatever challenges might come my way. I did not know what I would do with my life, but I looked forward to moving out into the wide world beyond Jasper, Dubois County, and southern Indiana. Wherever I would go, I would bring all these episodes, these people and places, these ripest moments, with me. No matter how far I would go or what I would do, I would always come back to my origins. Where I began is where I would return.

42

Invitation to a Family Picnic

Now that we've come this far, I realize it's time for a family picnic. You, my friend, are invited. Why don't you bring your brothers and sisters, your children and theirs? Also bring your parents and grandparents. I bet they'd love to get out, even if they walk slow and need a cane or walker. You know they would have some stories to tell about what their childhood was like. Talk to all of these people. I bet they'd love to come to the picnic. Nobody likes to be left out.

I talked to my cousin Mike Schmitt, who now owns the lake where we used to have those wonderful Schmitt family gatherings on Sunday. He built a log cabin there and dredged the lake after it became contaminated by fertilizer and spray that drained into the water from the neighbor's cornfield. Anyway, Mike says the water is now clean, we can swim in it, and the fish have come back. So bring your kids and a good fishing pole. Bring something to eat that can be shared with everybody. Bring something to drink: soft drinks, juice, beer, and chocolate milk. Somebody can bring a good radio that we'll plug in and turn up loud. We can use Aunt Frieda Hoffman's "cabin," that old bus that has the gas stove inside, for warming up dishes for the potluck. It gets pretty hot in the cabin in the summer, but we can roll down the windows.

The Schmitts, Uncle Alfred, my godfather, will come over from the farm later, with Aunt Elizabeth. Pat and Frank, the oldest sons, probably won't show, as they are always so busy with their chores and might not have the time to stop working and sit around with "city folk" like us. Funny, I always thought of "Chasper" as a small town. Mike, so handy with anything mechanical, especially vehicles of any kind, always likes to talk to us and will come, along with his quiet but smiling sister, Mary Ann.

Look, here come blonde Aunt Betty Schwartz, Dots' baby sister, who has such a Louisville "y'all" accent, and her family. Hear that, Uncle Louie Schwartz, that old devil, still calls her "Babe!" Out of the car tumble Donna and Johnnie and Jimmie. And not far behind them comes another car from Louisville, the Prechtels: Aunt Stella, Mom's sister who looks so much like her in every way, but who sounds a little different because she married a Louisville guy, Freddie Prechtel, and she's also got that "y'all" accent going. And their brood tumbles out of the car, I don't know if I can remember the names of even my first cousins, but I remember beautiful Mary Frances; pretty and plucky

Phyllis, who is my age; young Freddie, who is incredibly tall; and Bill, Gene, and Ray. It's so nice when the "Louis-will" folks, as Grandma calls them, come "on down," as we say, even though Dubois County is about as far south as Louisville, and in one sense we're as "southern" as they are, though we are Hoosiers and damned proud of it. We can beat their butts in basketball any time.

All of the Louisville Schmitts come up to say hello to Grandma, whose land this is, and ask how she's doing. We know, we live here, but we always check.

And look over there, Aunt Frieda got up early, went fly fishing in the back lake, and is bringing back to her cabin to fry a string of fish whose scales glint in the summer sunlight. What a grin she has on her face! Remember when Uncle Otto, her husband, died so young of a liver disease? What a tease he was. He used to call his little boy, cousin Charles, "Humpty Dumpty" and "The Little Boy Who Pees in the Snow." Wasn't it fun to watch the World Series at the Hoffman's house before the rest of us got television? How I loved to go there and watch the Yankees and the Brooklyn Dodgers (no, we'll not let them betray us by moving out to the traitorous West Coast) or the New York Giants in the World Series. Remember those Sunday afternoons when we watched television (*The Lone Ranger*) in their den, with logs burning in the fireplace, and Aunt Frieda serving hotdogs in buns, with baked beans, potato chips, and Coca Cola in those thick, green, glass bottles? The ice cream she and Uncle Otto made on the patio was so unbelievably creamy and delicious we always asked if they could please make us some more. Aunt Frieda has come a long way since she lost Uncle Otto, and having this cabin on the lake has been good for her, Otto Jr.; Jim, who is my age; Sara; and Charles. Aunt Frieda can fish with the best—man, woman, or beast.

Aunt Lucy and Uncle Bill Schmitt are already here. Howard, who always has one of those rum-soaked Crook cigars in his mouth, is home working on the farm. Ken is probably out with his high school friends hot rodding around in that souped-up car of his with the rumbling glass-pack muffler and the hot tires that so often lay rubber. But Alan, my squirrel- and rabbit-hunting buddy, is here getting his fishing gear ready. Nancy, always one of my favorites, is making terrific drawings of her Kentucky cousins in the shade of the maple tree beside the cabin. Also here is quiet Connie and jabbery Janie, the one with the broad smile. Aunt Lucy is greeting everybody and laughing at Uncle Louie's latest joke. And wouldn't you know it, Uncle Bill, who's been doing those isometric excerises, has stripped off his shirt to show off his bulging biceps and is about to do the old look-at-me-stand-on-my-head cool uncle routine.

"Hey, Schmittie, chust who you tryin' to impress?" somebody yells.

Over there in a chair with a big grin on his face is my Dad, Clarence, with a bottle of beer in his hand and a grin on his face. He's the one who taunted his brother-

ABOVE: Uncle Bill Schmitt entertains the clan while his son Howard smokes a stogy and daughter Nancy observes the goings-on. RIGHT: Grandma Schmitt offers birthday cake to anyone who comes to the picnic at her lake.

in-law. Dad's listening to a baseball game on the radio
and shooting the breeze with Uncle Louie, who shoots
more bull than breeze. They're both happy. Dad has been
so much better since he came back from the hospital. I
remember that first time he drove the car after he came
back. It was so tense when we set out to drive down to the
farm, which is down the road from this lake on "the other
forty acres," as Mom calls it. Remember how quiet we all
were as we drove along? Wasn't it unbelievable that when
we were driving west on Sixth Street and came to the end
of the high school, that pickup truck came rolling down the
hill without a driver and bumped the back fender? We saw
it coming, could not stop it, but nobody was hurt and the
car was easily fixed. It seemed like that scene was in slow
motion. Some little kids put the pickup in neutral, released
the brake, and let it roll. "The little dickens!" as Mom
called them. Yes, this picnic is so good for Dad.

Where the devil is Ed, that little shyster? He must have
run off with my rod and reel and my best lures to show me
he can catch a bigger, better fish. He must be down there
around the back corner of the lake with Huck Finn, who
also loves to fish, even though he just dangles a cane pole
with a worm for catfish. Nothin' fancy about Huck, you
see. Don't we all have a friend like Huck when we're kids?
He's such a good kid, even though he knows how to get into
trouble. He "learned" me how to crawl out the window at
night to go out to that old haunted house on the outskirts
of town with my cousin Marlene Kunkel and others. And

where's little Lenny, my younger brother? There he is, little "booger," running around in circles in the grass. I think he wants to go swimming and I'm about to join him. And little sis Mary Lou, "Toots," as we call her? She's hanging around with Mom, who is dishing out some fried chicken and potato salad and singing "You Are My Sunshine," her favorite song next to "The Tennessee Waltz." She and Dad went to the Smokies for their honeymoon, you know. Wasn't I born almost exactly nine months after Mom and Dad got married in the Saint Peter and Paul Cathedral in Indianapolis? They tried to elope, but brother Edgar and sisters Verena and Louise Krapf, all of whom lived in Indy, wouldn't let that happen and notified Grandma Mary and Grandpa Benno Krapf and sister Flora Schwinghamer, who was soon to become my godmother. They all drove to Indianapolis from Dubois County and had a little celebration at Aunt Verena's and Uncle Jerry's house at 1402 North Livingston Street near the Indianapolis Motor Speedway.

So you never know what you might find out at a picnic. When families get together, everybody eats and has something to drink, and you all start to talk. Being together with family stirs and stokes the old memory machine and times and places and people start to come back, and when it starts, "you kin hardly stop it," as Huck Finn says. Just let 'er rip, he once told me when we were fishing in the Patoka, near my favorite squirrel-hunting woods where Queenie and Ike and I would stand in the spring, when the world was young and so full of promise. Everything, including the river, rippled with potential.

So I did let 'er rip, in a manner of speaking, and I hope you have enjoyed coming along. I guess there's always more to tell, there are more people I know driving down the road to come to this picnic, and now you know who many of them are, but maybe it's time for me to stop and you to start telling your story. To tell you the truth, I was sometimes amazed by how much I remembered, how much was down there, how much came back and up into the light. All these people, all these incidents, all these places, are a part of who I was and what I became. I feel mighty good about what I have done in telling you all this and am so glad you were there to listen. Good luck, see you around, take care, be well, and tell everybody hello.